DIY Projects & Gift Ideas for Father's Day

By: Do It Yourself Nation

Copyright © 2015 by Do It Yourself Nation

All rights reserved. No part of this book may be reproduced in any form without permission in writing from the author. Reviewers are able to quote brief passages in reviews.

Disclaimer

This document is geared towards providing exact and reliable information in regards to the topic and issue covered. The publication is sold with the idea that the publisher is not required to render accounting, officially permitted, or otherwise, qualified services. If advice is necessary, legal or professional, a practiced individual in the profession should be ordered.

- From a Declaration of Principles which was accepted and approved equally by a Committee of the American Bar Association and a Committee of Publishers and Associations.

In no way is it legal to reproduce, duplicate, or transmit any part of this document in either electronic means or in printed format. Recording of this publication is strictly prohibited and any storage of this document is not allowed unless with written permission from the publisher. All rights reserved.

The information provided herein is stated to be truthful and consistent, in that any liability, in terms of inattention or otherwise, by any usage or abuse of any policies, processes, or directions contained within is the solitary and utter responsibility of the recipient reader. Under no circumstances will any legal responsibility or blame be held against the publisher for any reparation, damages, or monetary loss due to the information herein, either directly or indirectly.

Respective authors own all copyrights not held by the publisher.

The information herein is offered for informational purposes solely, and is universal as so. The presentation of the information is without contract or any type of guarantee assurance.

The trademarks that are used are without any consent, and the publication of the trademark is without permission or backing by the trademark owner. All trademarks and brands within this book are for clarifying purposes only and are the owned by the owners themselves, not affiliated with this document.

Introduction

Is Father's Day almost here and you can't figure out what to give your dad? Are you tired of giving the same old socks, shirts or ties to your dad for every occasion? Do you want to try something different? Are you looking for a large collection of fresh and unique gift ideas for your Dad?

Would you like to put a smile on your dad's face by giving a special handmade gift, specifically designed for him? Or have you previously spent a lot of money buying those men's gifts and found them not to be worth all the money? Have you wished you could make a similar gift from locally available raw materials?

Do your siblings or workmates think you are less creative or even to some extent ignorant because of your inability to create wonderful gifts for your father? If you are in such a situation, this book is all that you need. You can get all the information you need to design and give unique presents for Father's Day.

To show how much you care for your Father, you can adopt the different ideas suggested here. The ideas include Dad-focused artwork, gifts for the office, and photo-theme crafts. There are also gift ideas for electronics, clothes and accessories, home décor and food gifts just to mention a few. This is the only book you need to put a smile on your dad's face on Father's Day.

About This Book

This DIY project book is divided into six chapters, with each highlighting a different gift category as illustrated here:

The first chapter suggests gadgets and accessories that you can design this Father's Day. The next chapter covers various ways of improving your dad's house in the home décor section. The third chapter helps you figure out the kind of clothes and related accessories for Father's Day. The fourth chapter reveals ways in which you can prepare food for your dad in easy to follow steps. The following chapter suggests how you can make body and cleaning products such as soaps, creams, and bath salts. The last chapter has other miscellaneous gifts that you can try. The table of contents below gives a clear view of what you can expect to gain from this book.

Table of Contents

Introduction	1
About This Book	2
Chapter 1: Electronics and Accessories	**6**
Fashionable cord rolls	6
Laptop riser for bed	9
Electronic speaker from scratch	12
PVC pipe clock	16
DIY water battery	20
DIY spider rifle	24
Chapter 2: Home Décor	**29**
Firewood tote	29
Mustache mug tutorial	30
Tres lamp	31
DIY wooden bungee organizer	36
DIY floppy disk planters	38
DIY Scrabble Frame	41
Chapter 3: Clothes and Accessories	**43**
Necktie eyeglasses case	43
Hand warmer DIY	45
No-sew slipper socks	47
Car shirt gift	49
Stamped leather tie clip	50
Lego cufflinks	52

    Adjustable unisex apron   56

Chapter 4: Food Gift Ideas   **70**

    Jack and Coke cake   70

    Veggie fries for men   73

    Beef jerky   75

    Remote control cookies   77

    Big batch barbecue rub   79

    Homemade honey curry mustard   80

Chapter 5: Pampering Gift Ideas   **83**

    Rosemary mint shaving cream   83

    Black and tan beer soap   84

    Eucalyptus and vanilla bath salts   88

    DIY fragrance made with vodka   89

    Chamomile & neroli beer soap   91

Chapter 6: Miscellaneous Crafts Ideas   **93**

    Shrinky Dink gift   93

    Tripod camping stool   95

    Bicycle frame lunch bag   100

    Simple stitched vinyl wallet   103

    Homemade leather wallet   105

    Swiss Army key ring   111

Conclusion   **120**

Key Takeaways from this Book   **121**

How to Put This Information into Action   **122**

Preview of Essential Oils and Aromatherapy: A Beginner's Guide to Making Essential Oils to Improve Your Mental and Physical Well-Being   123

More Books You Might Like   125

Your Free Bonus   126

Chapter 1:
Electronics and Accessories

Let's start with amazing electronics and accessories gift ideas for your dad.

Fashionable cord rolls

What you'll need

- Pencil
- Matte cutting board
- Metal ruler
- X-ACTO knife
- Snap buttons
- ¼ yard leather, real or fake

How to make

Create three cord rolls ranging from small to medium and large. The small cord roll is useful for holding wall chargers for phones, while the medium cord can be used to hold headphones, phone chargers, USB cords or other auxiliary cords. The larger cords are good for holding Jambox chargers, laptop adapters, headphones and others.

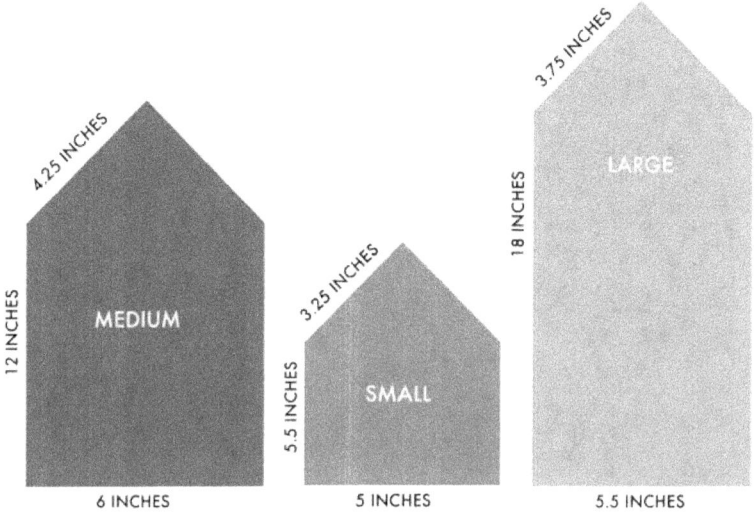

From the illustration, measure and cut out your piece to size. If using fake leather, it's even easier to cut using an X-ACTO knife and a metal ruler to get very straight edges.

Cut some small pieces that should act as your loops for the cords and then arrange the cords and charger in a row. Use a pencil to mark the places where the rolls would meet. Ensure you do this when all the cords are in place.

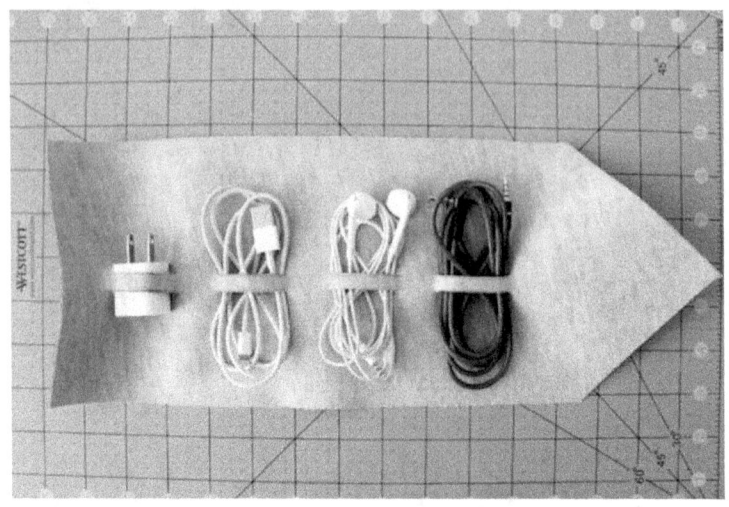

Now push the snap buttons through and the secure the two ends as shown here:

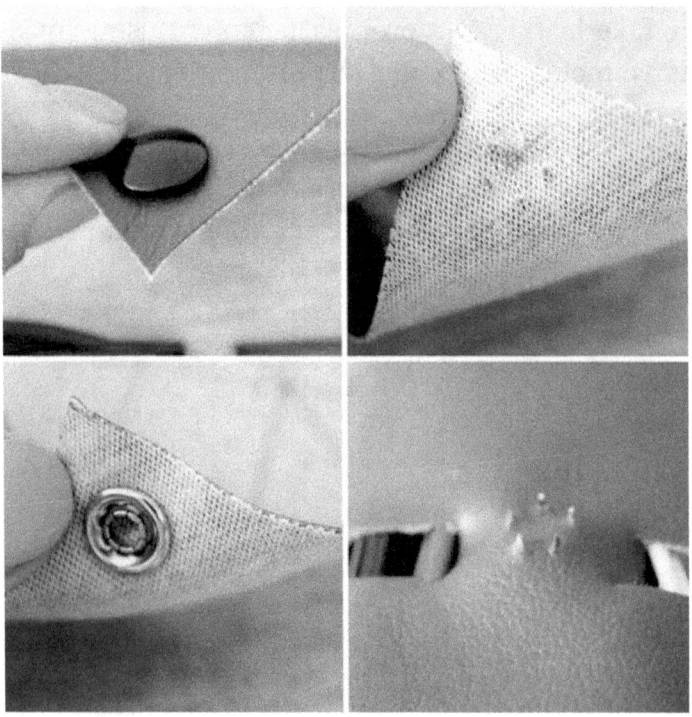

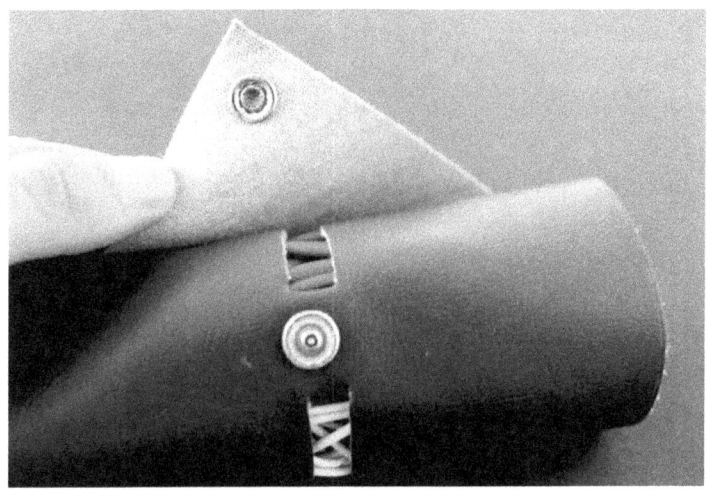

Repeat the procedure to get all the three different sized cord rolls for your Father's Day gift

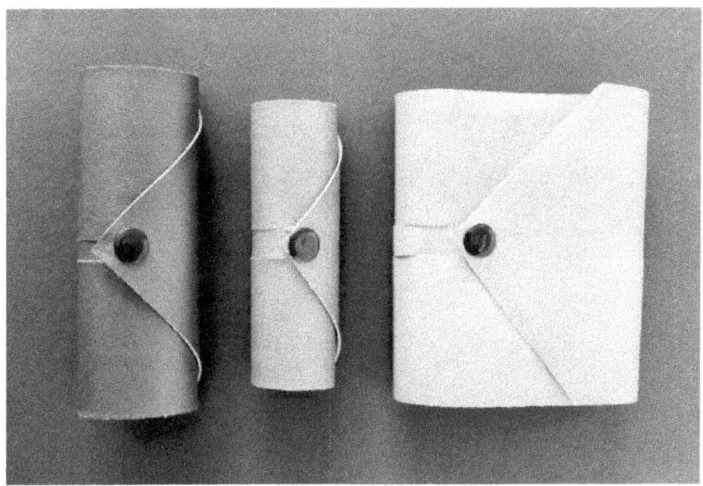

Laptop riser for bed

What you'll need

- Cable tacks
- 1 extension cord

- 2 screw-in towel hooks

- Saw

- Bent plywood stool, e.g. IKEA Benjamin

How to make

Start by determining the actual size (height) of your riser. In order to determine the size, you need to know what you will be using it for. For instance, if it is for watching movies, you may want it to be around 4 inches. To prevent splintering on the cut end, just put a little masking tape and then use a saw to cut.

Now screw the 2 towel hooks on every end of the sides, ensuring that the curved bottoms are facing in. Use the cable tacks to attach the extension cord to the inside.

For storage, wrap a cable around the towel hooks.

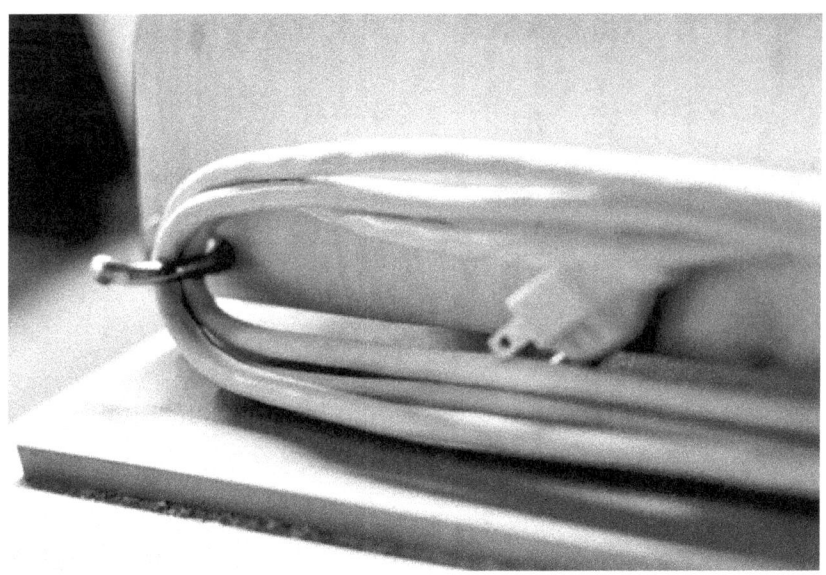

Electronic speaker from scratch

What you'll need

- iPod touch or radio
- Some alligator clips.
- Sticky tape and Popsicle sticks
- AC or DC battery/ cylinder smaller than a cup
- Some copper wire
- A 3.5mm headphone jack
- A small magnet
- A Styrofoam/paper cup

How to make

Make your copper wire into a neat circle, and have the ends hang off 3-4cm. Wrap the copper wire around a battery and hold it in place as you wrap the two ends around the coil to hold it in shape. Tape the coil down onto the top of the cup.

On the two ends of the copper wire, put some wire or alligator clips and then place a stripped 3.5mm headphone jack on the other ends.

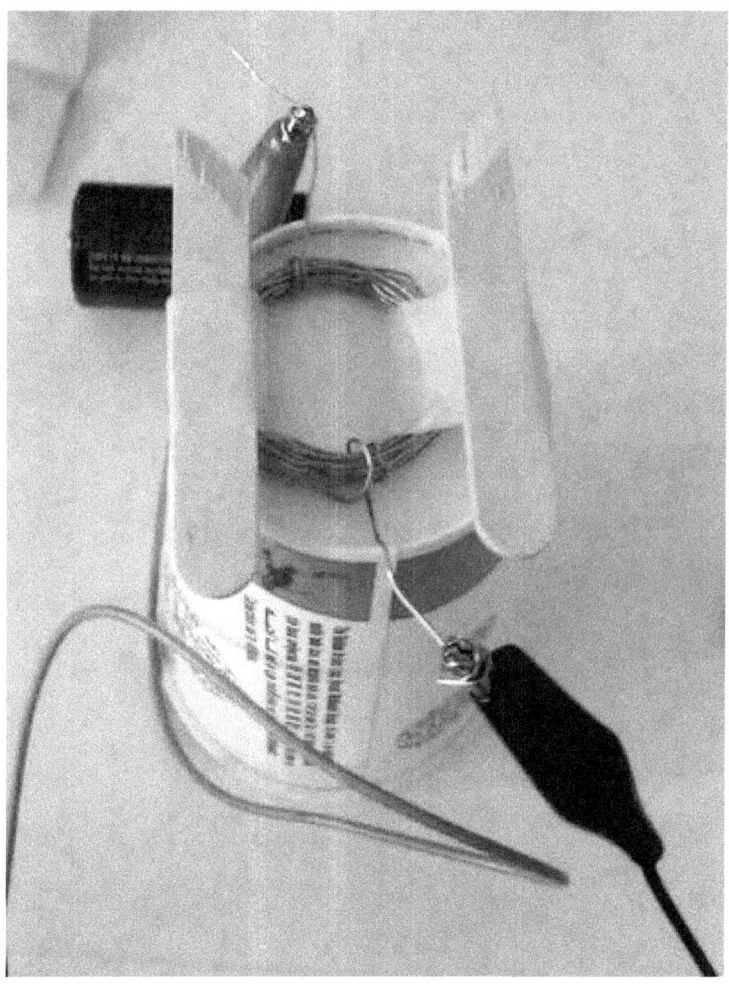

Now tape the Popsicle onto your cup so that it makes a frame for your magnet.

Pop your magnet on the frame, positioning it directly over the copper coil, then plug into your radio or iPod player.

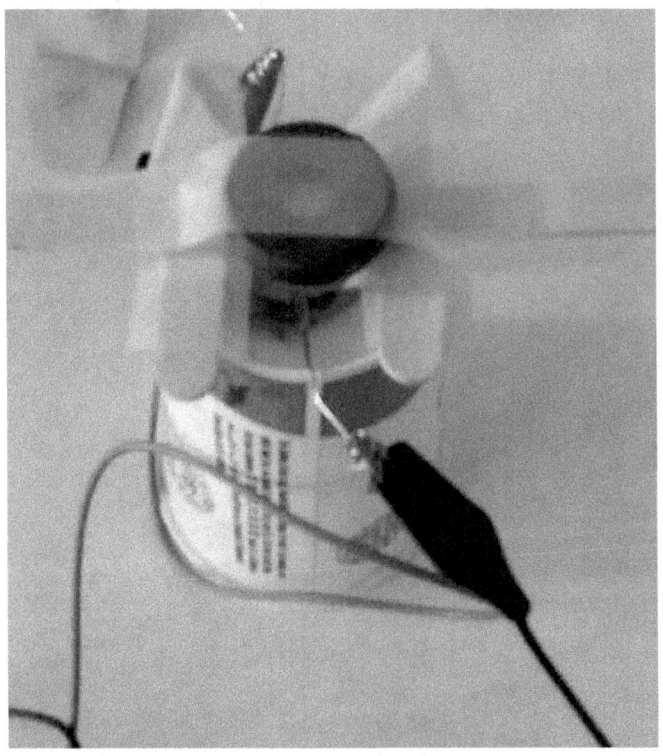

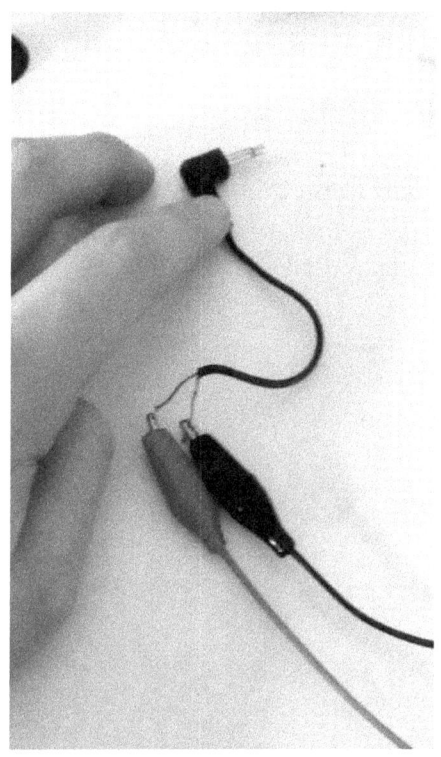

If your speaker is not working, remove the Popsicle sticks and position the magnet almost on top of the coil. Also, obtain a more powerful magnet and a radio instead of an iPod. When well designed, this can be a fully functional speaker!

PVC pipe clock

What you'll need

- Double-sided foam tape
- AA battery
- AA battery holder
- Electrical tape
- Spray paint
- Cardboard
- PVC pipe
- Clock
- Marker
- WD-40 (or rubbing alcohol)
- X-ACTO knife
- Scissors

How to make

When buying your clock, make sure that the round clear plastic cover on your clock is around the same size as your pipe. From your clock, remove the clear plastic cover and then wrap an electric tape around it. This allows you to get a good fit between your clock and PVC pipe.

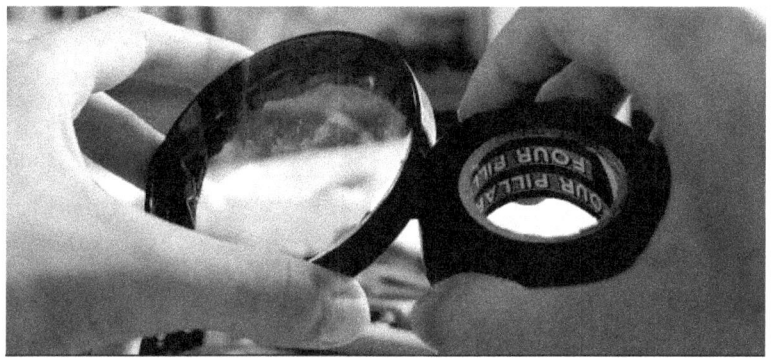

When done, cut the tape off and test if it tightly fits into your pipe. Now cut off the extra tape after finishing with the fitting.

From a thin cardboard piece, trace two circles that have similar measurements to your clock cover, and cut them out. The circles should tightly fit into the pipe.

Spray-paint one of the cardboard circles black to mount the clock interface and to make the clock face. Then cut a U-shaped tab in the other circle to form a lid that prevents the battery falling out. You will use the U-tab when pulling out your clock's bottom cover to modify clock settings.

To solder the battery holder, locate the positive and negative terminals from your clock. You need one AA battery for ordinary clock functions or two if you need alarm and LED functions. Test if the clock can function.

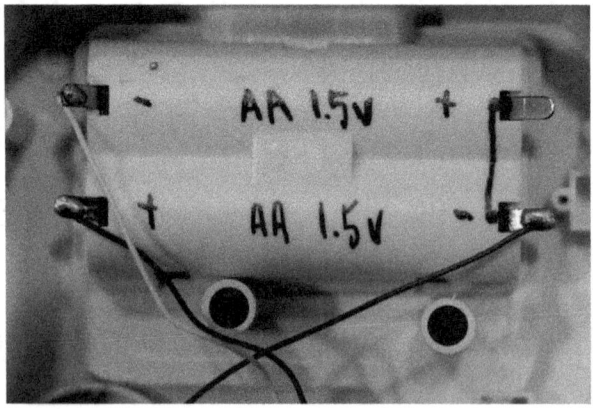

Through the center of the spray-painted cardboard, make a hole and place a few pieces of double-sided foam tape on the clock mechanism. Attach the two together.

Onto the axel of the clock, mount the clock's hands and put the battery, LED, and alarm inside the pipe. Fit the clock into the PVC pipe and make the required time adjustments. Now tightly push the cover into the pipe. Wipe the interior of the cover before putting it in.

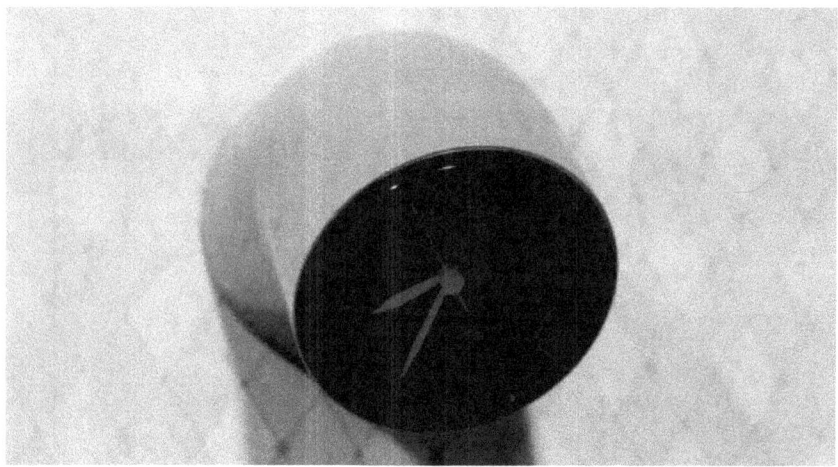

Finally, push the bottom cover (that with U-tab on it), making sure it's tight and well laid.

DIY water battery

What you'll need

- 6 pieces of zinc
- 6 pieces of copper
- 6 plastic bottles, 1 liter
- Clamp cables
- LED lights (low voltage)
- Water
- Zinc sulfate
- Copper sulfate

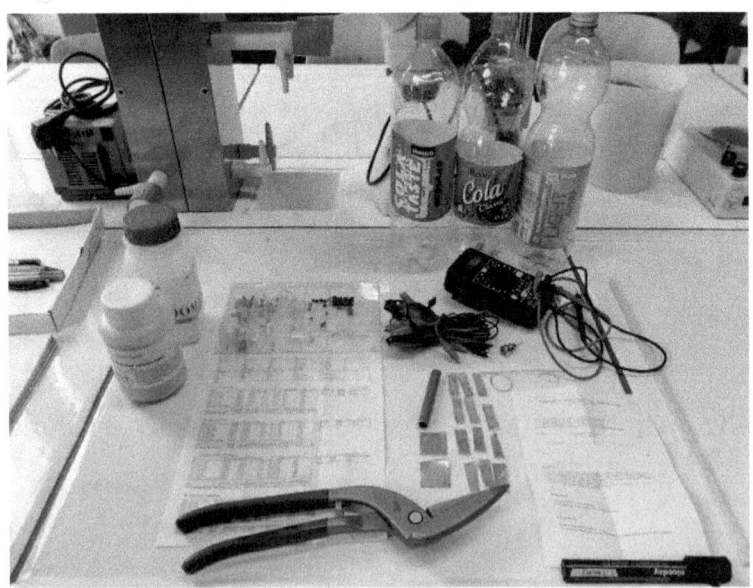

How to make

Fill the 6 bottles with water, and place them in a wooden frame for easier moving. Cut the copper and zinc into 6 pieces each and put them in every bottle.

Now to the most technical part; fill your bottles and connect the anodes and cathodes. Add 20 grams of copper sulfate to the upper left bottle and 20 grams zinc sulfate to the lower left bottle. Add the same amount of zinc sulfate to the upper center bottle and copper sulfate to the lower center bottle. Lastly, add 20 grams copper sulfate to the upper right bottle and zinc sulfate to the lower right bottle. Each of the bottles produces 2 volts.

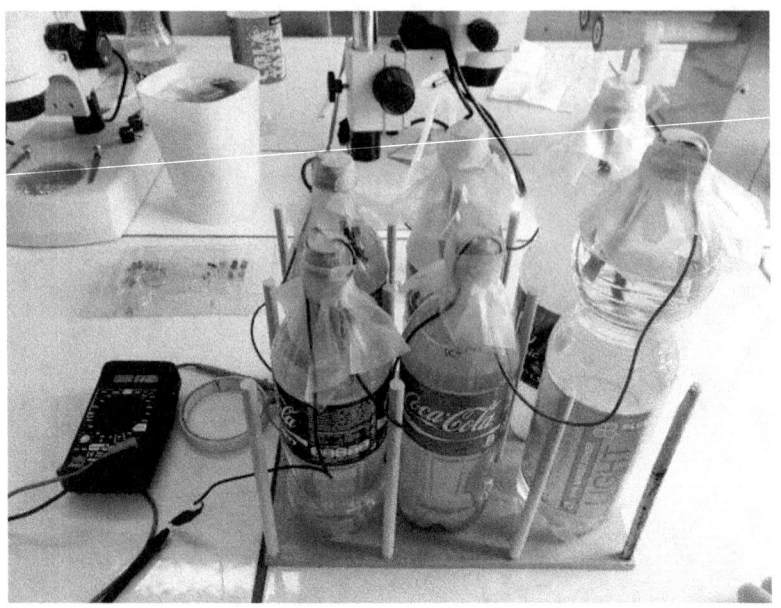

3. Connect the copper to red wire and zinc on the other side to obtain positive (+) and negative (-) terminals. Connect the zinc to black wire and copper on the other end. Begin at the first bottle with copper and end at the other bottle with zinc. Begin with red wire at the second bottle then end in the next bottle where you'll begin with a black wire. The connection creates an electric circuit. The clamp cables should not touch water.

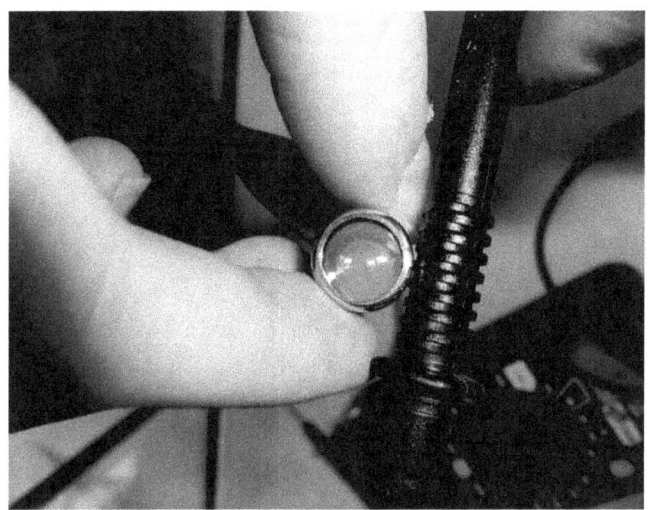

You should end up having a red wire from the first bottle and a black one from the last. Cover the bottle necks using rubber or plastic to avoid evaporation. To measure the voltage, use a voltmeter, or test using a LED. The picture above shows a 12-volt LED burning.

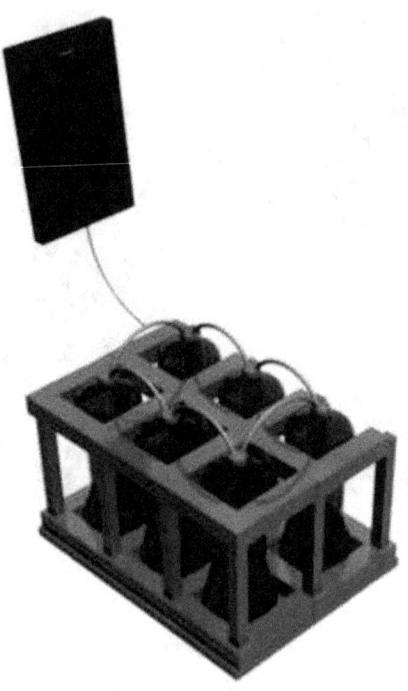

You can use clamps to connect the battery to a charging wire to charge a low-powered object like a cell phone.

DIY spider rifle

What you'll need

- Small thin semi-rigid plastic
- Can of compressed air
- 70mm hose clamp
- 1" PVC end cap
- 1"x½" PVC coupler
- ½" CPVC 90° elbow fitting

- ½" CPVC 45° elbow fitting
- ½" CPVC T-fitting
- ½" CPVC coupler
- 5' or 10' length of ½" CPVC plumbing pipe

Optional:

- Can of spray clear coat
- Can of spray paint
- 1 can of multipurpose PVC cement
- 1 can of PVC primer
- PVC cement or hot glue

How to make

1. Cut the ½ inch CPVC pipe into 4 lengths of 18 inches, two pieces of 4 inches each, and ¾ inches.

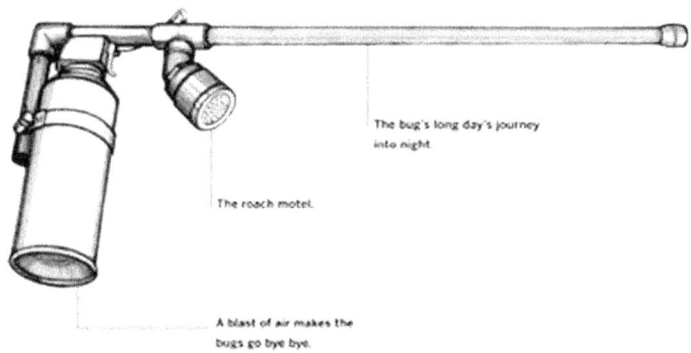

The bug's long day's journey into night.

The roach motel.

A blast of air makes the bugs go bye bye.

Cut a slit lengthwise ½ inch from the end in one of the 4-inch pieces of the pipe. Ensure that the slit is about ¾ inches long and goes completely through the pipe. The slit is useful in clamping the can of the compressed spider rifle. You may drill a small number of pilot holes through the pipe and then use a utility knife to cut the rest out. Take care not to let the knife slip, and ensure you wear a respirator or dusk mask.

Drill a hole into the center of the CPVC T-fitting using an R (0.339" / 9 mm) drill bit. The hole should go in the can of compressed air. Other sizes of drill bits are OK, though you may need to rim out a little if you use a smaller bit or fill gaps using hot glue if you use a larger bit.

Make as many drill holes as you can in the one-inch end cap, to allow air through. Then trace and cut out the T-fitting stop valve, which can be cut out of any semi-rigid plastic. Try coffee lids, which are thick enough, easy to trace on, and evenly cut.

Get a piece of ½ inch pipe, make it stand on top of the plastic and then trace around it using a Sharpie marker. Use scissors to cut out the circle and then put in the T-fitting. To make it fit fully, just cut small amounts, taking care not to cut too much, and cause it to slide through. The top should rest up against the ridge near the middle.

Now push the 4 inches of pipe that doesn't have the slit firmly into the T-fitting that has the plastic stop. To the end of the 4-inch pipe, connect the 90° elbow and then push the ¾-inch pipe into the bottom of the T-fitting.

Now connect the 45° fitting to the ¾-inch pipe and then connect the other 4-inch pipe to the 90° elbow fitting. Join the ½-inch to the 1-inch coupler to the end of the 45° elbow. Then connect the barrel to the T-fitting.

To the end of the barrel, attach the ½-inch coupler and then prime and cement all joints. Alternatively, you can use any other adhesive of your choice.

Cut in half the ½-inch coupler at the end of the barrel, using the seam on the coupler as your guide. Through the handle, insert the clamp and then tighten partially. Twist the 1-inch end cap onto the bottom of the 1-inch coupler.

You can paint your spider rifle if desired, and then wait for the paint to dry out. Once dry, insert a plastic air tube from the can of compressed air into the top of your T-fitting.

Now slide the can of compressed air through the clamp, which makes the top rest properly against your rifle. Ensure you tighten the clamp to make it snug, without over-tightening, since the can is under pressure.

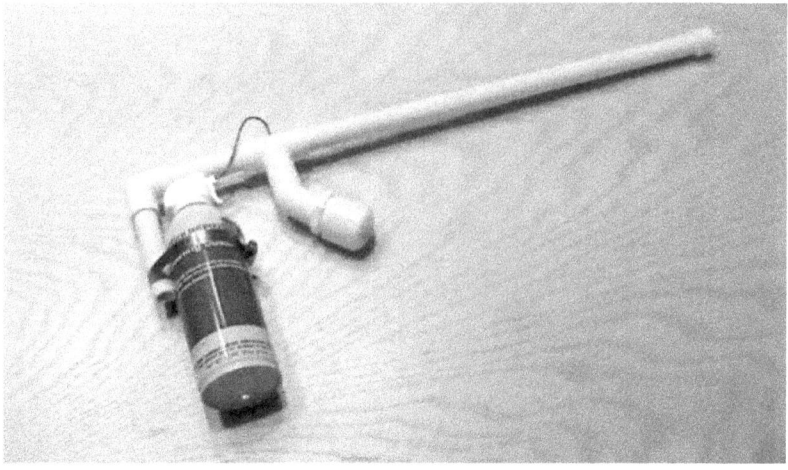

To complete, connect the air tube to the can of air. To use, just point the barrel of the rifle near spiders or other insects and then press the trigger. The air is forced through the bottom of the drilled PVC end cap. As the T-fitting is blocked on the side joined to the handle, a vacuum is created in the barrel by forcing air downward and out the bottom. The vacuum created draws the insect inward into the drilled 1-inch end cap acting as the 'catch'.

Chapter 2: Home Décor

Firewood tote

What you'll need

- Canvas
- Flannel
- Sewing machine
- Cutting tools such as scissors

How to make

Start by cutting canvas and a flannel measuring 20" x 40" and then sew along the sides using right sides facing (RSF). Cut out a rectangle that measures 6x8" from the center of the short sides and then sew around each rectangle.

Through one of the open ends, turn right sides out (RSO). To do this, fold the ends towards the inside, turning the raw edges under. Now sew over each of the edges twice.

Then slide small branches into the loops (or 25-inch long dowel rods). Carry the two sticks in the center with the flannel on the exterior.

Mustache mug tutorial

What you'll need

- Gel and pen
- Pebeo porcelain
- Sharpie marker
- Mug

How to make

On your porcelain mug, use a sharpie marker to draw a mustache. Then, use the Pebeo pen to trace around the edges of your drawn mustache. Now use your Pebeo gel stain to fill the mustache. To get the best quality, you'll need to apply a couple of coats.

Finally, follow the stain guidelines. For instance, some need baking at specific temperatures for a certain time. After this, you can fill the decorated mug with candies or a drink and offer your gift.

Tres lamp

What you'll need

- Electrical plug
- Electrical cord
- Lamp socket (E26)
- Light bulb (E26)
- Large scrap cardboard from 14" square
- Natural fiber cording 54"

- Three ½-inch diameter wooden dowel rods, cut to 20" length
- Electrical tape
- Sandpaper
- Wire cutters
- Utility knife
- Hand saw
- Protractor
- Scissors
- Pencil
- Ruler

How to make

Start by making a cardboard template to help you keep the dowels in place as you work on the project. Measure out a 12-inch equilateral triangle using a ruler and protractor and then poke holes into the three points to erect the dowels.

Make the feet that will support your tripod structure and present a finished look for your tres lamp. Mark about ¼ inch from one end of each dowel using a pencil. To make the angled cuts meet in a straight line to those marks, use your handsaw to cut. Also, use a medium or low-grit sandpaper to clean up the ends of the dowels when done.

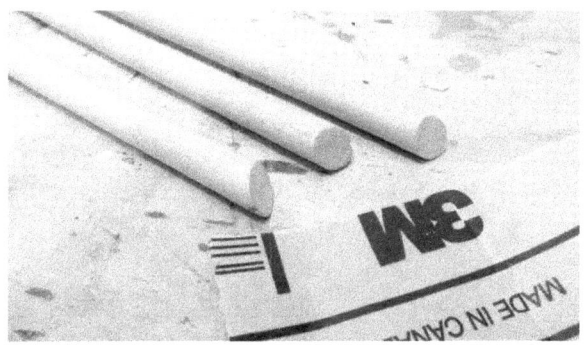

Make the notch to assist in creating a tripod structure using a single knot. Mark a line 5 inches from the top of a dowel. Then cut about 1/3 of the way deep, leaving the other two dowels untouched.

Wet the cord to help make the tripod sturdy (this only works on natural fiber cords). Do this by soaking under running water to allow the fibers expand. The cord need to remain taut during the wrapping exercise.

To start the wrap, pull your saturated cord down into your previously made notch and leave 8 inches slack on the right and left sides. Roll the dowel over the point of the other two dowels next to it.

Place the electrical cord at a particular spot, either between or on the top of the dowels. After this, wrap the long end of the cord on the cord or dowel bunch, about 4-5 times. Position the cord as you wrap, keeping it at medium tightness.

To erect the structure, get the template you had previously made and follow it to stand the cord and dowel upright. Ensure that the feet are facing away from the center, but sitting flush to the table surface and the cardboard.

Position the cord to the middle of the bunch from the original top position, and then tighten completely. When tightening, pay attention for any creaking sound, which signifies that the cord is taut enough.

Make a knot in order to secure the tripod structure, and then prepare the cord for connection to the terminal. You need electrical tape and wire cutters.

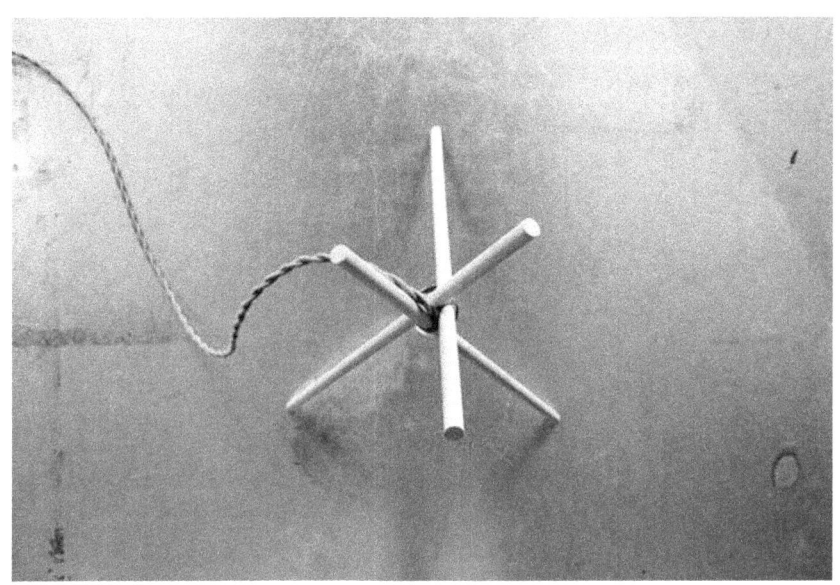

Adjust the height of the electrical cord based on your bulb length, and give it a firm tug in whatever direction. When securely in place, screw in the bulb, plug it in and then have your gift ready!

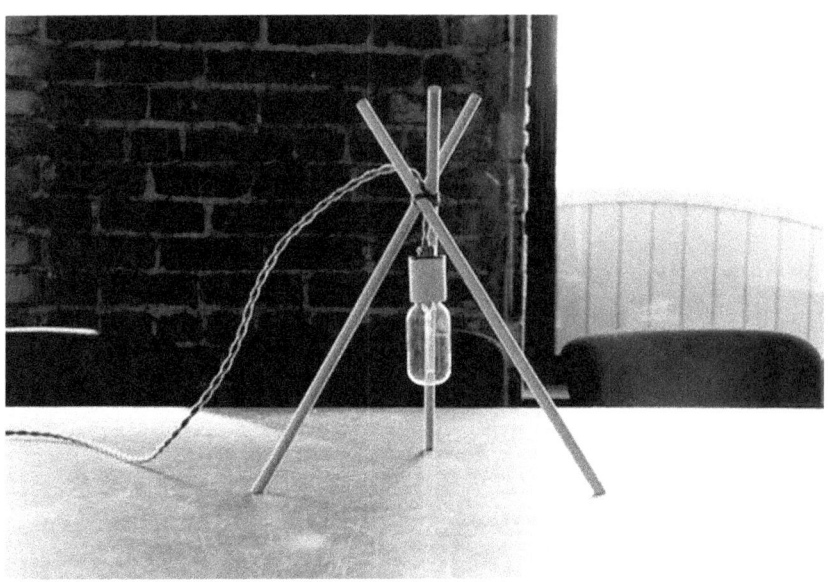

DIY wooden bungee organizer

What you'll need

- Hammer
- Stapler
- Lighter
- Drill
- Picture hanging kit
- 3 2-foot hobby boards
- Wood stain
- Bungee cords (red, yellow, and blue)

How to make

Ensure the area you are working on is properly ventilated due to the fumes from the wood stain. Into each hobby board, drill two holes using a drill bit that is thicker than the size of your bungee.

Use paper towel or rag to add wood stain and stain each piece of your wood. Allow the stained wood to rest for about 10 minutes.

Cut the hooks off the bungee cords and seal the ends using a lighter. This will help prevent the cords from fraying. Pull the cord through the hole you have drilled and then use a staple gun to fix it to your board. You may also use a regular stapler plus a hammer.

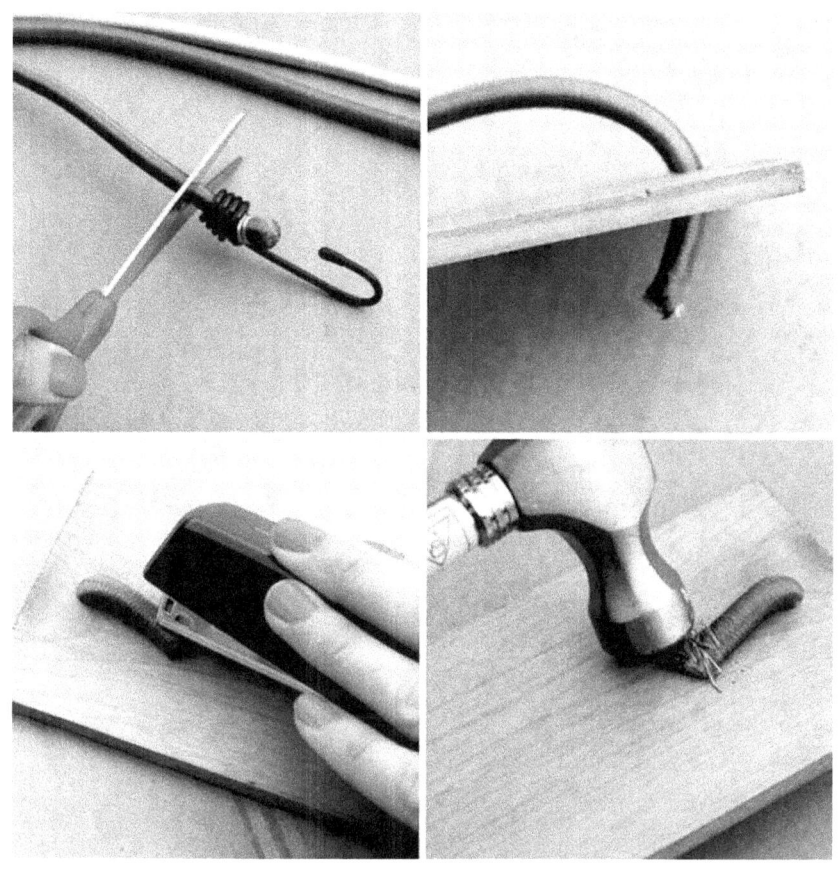

To add wire to the back of the caddy, use a standard picture hanging kit and then simply send your gift to be hanged.

DIY floppy disk planters

What you'll need

- Yogurt containers
- Seeds
- Soil
- Plants
- Hot glue or Marine Glue
- Floppy disks
- Scissors

How to make

Sort your floppy disks by color, and get five different planters with five disks per planter.

To make the planting box, heat up the hot glue and then squeeze a thin line onto the edge of a disk. Now attach the disk to the second disk's edge and continue with the process until you are done with all planters. Now glue four edges for the 5th disk and attach to complete the bottom.

If planting seeds from scratch, you may need to use an old yoghurt container first. Plant a few seeds in each container and then use floppy disk labels to name your plants if necessary. Also include directions on how to care for the plants.

When ready for transplanting, ensure that the leaves are in place, trim off the dead branches, and uproot harmful weeds. Water regularly. For the best experience, use a mix of hearty houseplants and succulents.

DIY Scrabble Frame

What you'll need

- Photos
- Photo frame
- Scrabble tiles
- Glue

How to make

Obtain a photo frame of the desired measurements and the background photo to use for the scrabble.

Search for the scrabble tiles you need to spell out different messages. Glue the tiles in position to complete the gift.

Chapter 3:
Clothes and Accessories

Necktie eyeglasses case

What you'll need

- A tie
- Glue
- Sewing machine

How to make

Cut your tie about 17 inches from the point. Your tie's interior is the part that will hold the glasses.

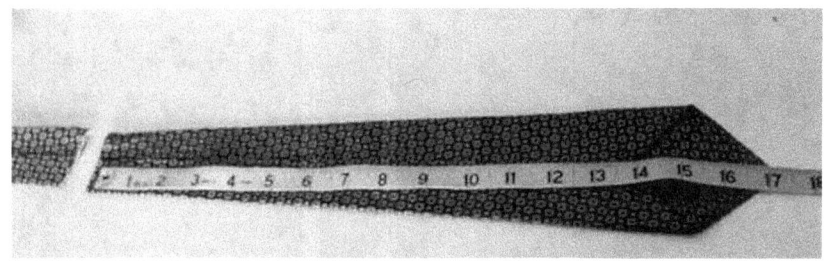

Apply glue or patch up any open or loose areas from the tie, and then fold the length of your tie over the back. As you do the folding, tuck in the very end about an inch to get an even better finished look.

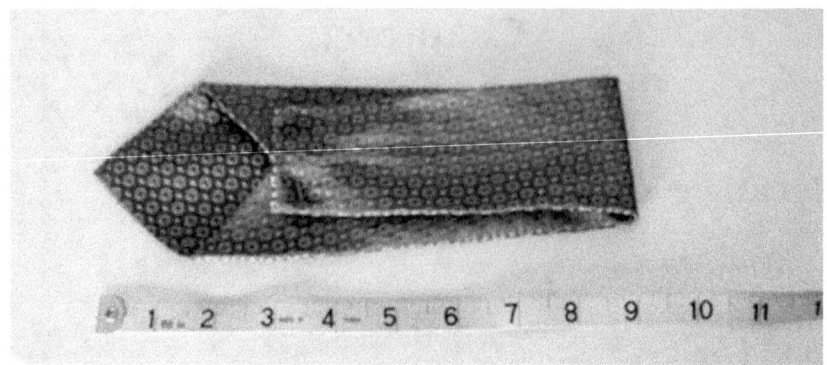

Then whip stitch along the sides and the tops, taking care not to sew the pouch closed. Now attach some Velcro to the tip and to the area that it will touch when closed. To avoid scratches with sunglasses, use the softer side of the Velcro where the eyeglasses will slide in.

Hand warmer DIY

What you'll need

- Thread
- Rice
- Long pins
- Sewing machine or needle
- Pinking shears, optional
- Fabric scissors
- Fat ¼ fabric

How to make

Cut 2 ¾- inch squares from your pattern using fabric scissors, about two patterns for each hand warmer.

Position 2 square fabrics with the wrong sides facing each other and then stitch ¼ inch seam around the exterior section. Ensure that you leave a 1½ inch opening and backstitch in the beginning and the end. (If you don't have pinking shears, just position the fabric right-sided together and then sew. Follow the sewing instructions and then turn them right.)

Now fill up to ¾ inch of the way up with rice, block the rice from falling out of the opening using a long pin, and then sew the opening. Trim the edges using pinking shears to help keep the fabric from fraying.

To use the hand warmers, they should first be warmed in the microwave for 20 seconds. Make sure they don't get very hot!

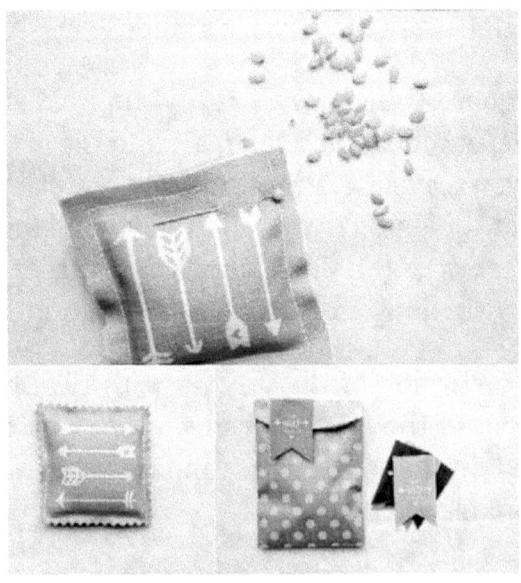

No-sew slipper socks

What you'll need

- Iron
- Fusible webbing
- Suede fabric
- Sewing pencil
- Scissors
- Pencil
- Scrap of cardboard
- Thick socks

How to make

Trace your feet using a pencil on a cardboard while wearing socks. Cut along the trace lines and then remove the socks.

Trace the new templates using a skewing pencil on a suede fabric and fusible webbing. The latter is a special material that can bond fabrics together. Now cut your template out then slide a cardboard template on the socks.

Place the template on a place where you want to iron new soles. Position the fusible webbing between the suede fabric and the sole of your sock following the guidelines from the webbing, iron and then remove the cardboard.

Car shirt gift

What you'll need

- Cars to drive on your map
- Fabric paint or fabric markers
- Printer and paper
- Plain white shirt

How to make

Sketch or draw a map to use, such as the one shown here, and then print.

Slide the printed paper in between the back and the front of your shirt. The back side should be facing up, to help prevent the paint from bleeding through to the front side.

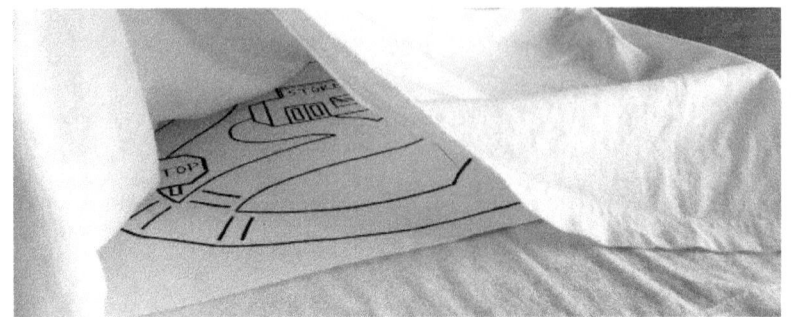

Start tracing your diagram using fabric paint or fabric markers. Use different inks and colors to create a better map with cars.

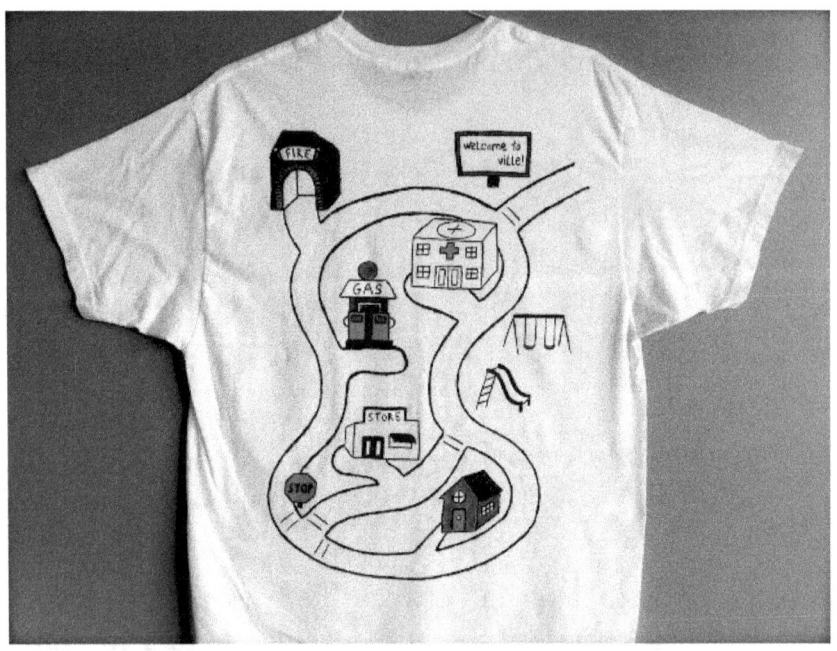

Stamped leather tie clip

What you'll need

- Hammer

- Letter and number punch set
- Strong glue
- Blank tie clip
- Craft knife
- Small piece of thick leather

How to make

Cut your leather to the size and shape of your tie clip. Decide the phrase or word you want to stamp on the leather using a metal punch set plus a hammer. You may need to experiment with a few sets of words.

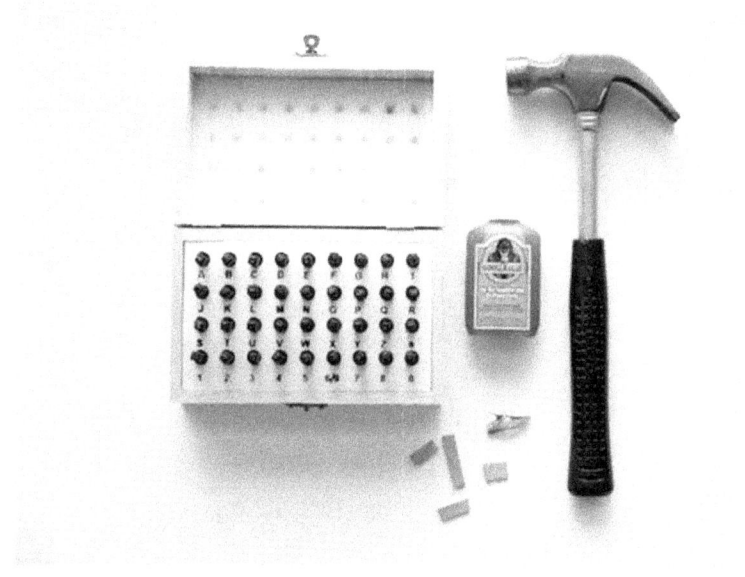

Glue the stamped piece of leather onto your clip, with the right side up when the tie clip is in use.

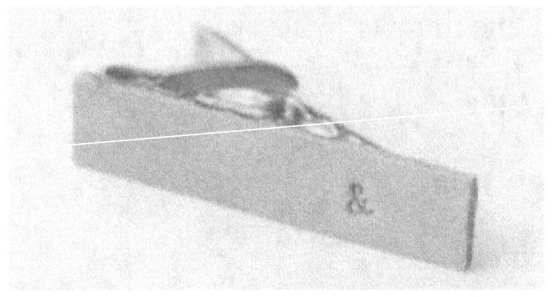

Lego cufflinks

What you'll need

- Stirrers for mixing epoxy

- Disposable containers

- 4 top Legos, square, thick or thin

- Cufflinks with 8mm pads

- Elmer's Super Fast Epoxy

How to make

To work with epoxy, be in a ventilated area and use only a small amount, as it dries very quickly. To mix epoxy, pour a little into a disposable container and stir. To apply a little glue to the cufflink, use the end of the stirring device. Just place over the circular bit in the middle of the back for a few minutes.

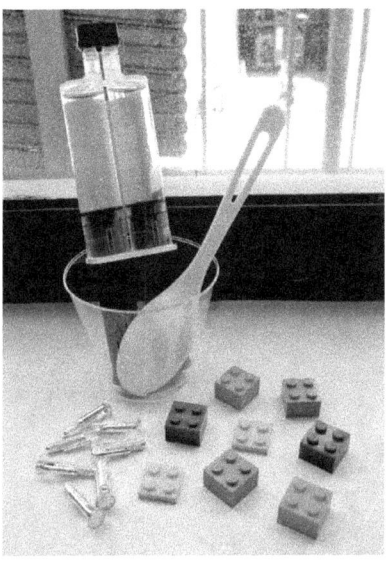

Repeat the application process for 4-5 cufflinks, press them down firmly, and mix up more epoxy for additional cuff links.

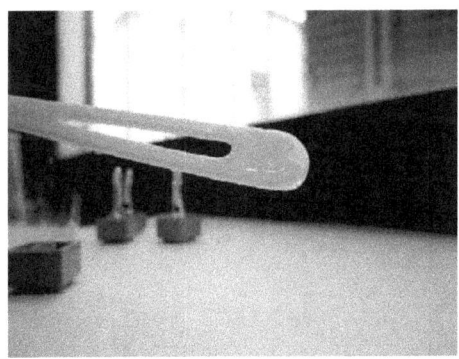

Allow the epoxy to cure for about 12-24 hours by hanging your cufflinks in a place safe from disturbance.

If you make any mistakes with epoxy, wipe it off immediately or you'll be forced to sand it off later. Also, ensure the glue does not get on your hands or clothes. You can use acetone nail polish remover to clean up epoxy.

Adjustable unisex apron

This is an amazing gift for the dad who loves cooking.

What you'll need

- 100% cotton thread in color 3260
- 3 yards of 30mm twill tape in ecru
- ½ yard of linen blend solid in lavender
- 1 ¼ yards of Ecrulet herringbone in grey

How to make

Start by marking and cutting the pattern. Then press the main body fabric in half lengthwise, selvedge to selvedge. Once done, trim the top of the fabric in order to have a 90° angle with fold.

Make an inch vertical mark using an erasable marker or tailor's chalk at the top of the fabric, about 6.5 inches from the fold. This constitutes the mark A shown in the picture:

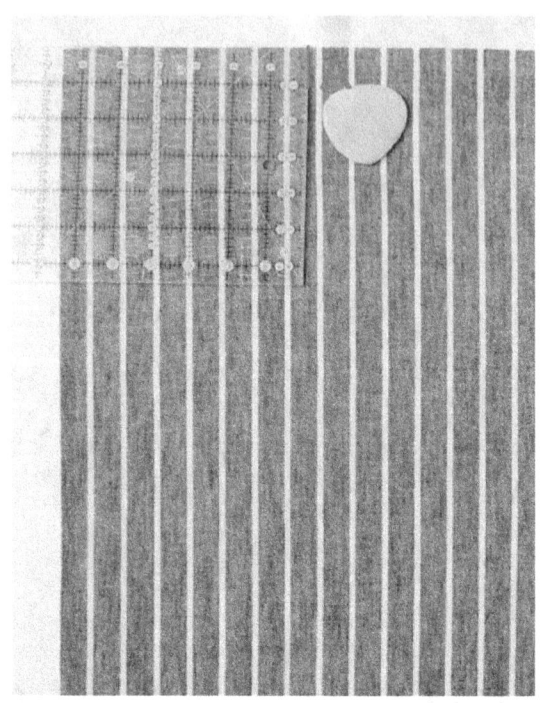

Along the fold, place a pin about 17 inches from the top of fabric, to constitute point B. Use a chalk to mark point C, 13 inches from the fold and directly perpendicular to point B. Finally mark point D, on the fold 20 inches below mark B.

Mark a point E about 20 inches vertically below point C and use chalk to join the marked lines using straight lines. Go from the bottom of mark A to mark C, diagonally; then go down to mark E and then over to D.

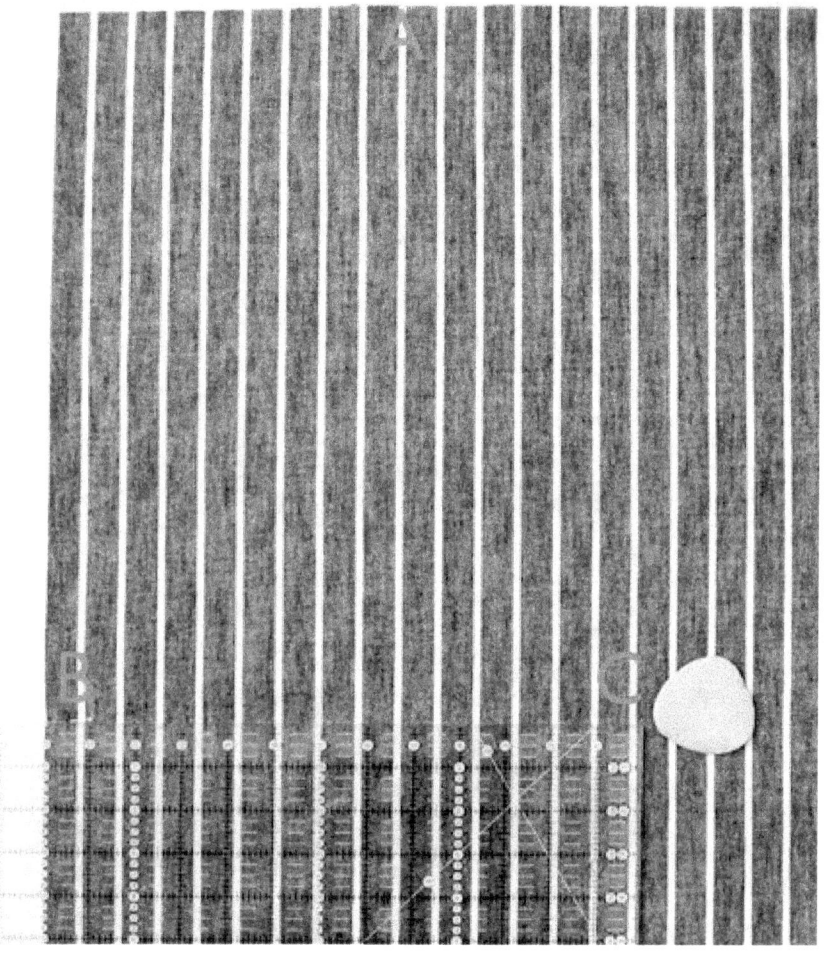

Then cut the apron along the mark lines. Cut a rectangular pattern measuring 17x20 inches, using stripes that run horizontally for the pocket.

To sew the apron, unfold from the main apron piece and hem the top and straight sides using a darker thread, by folding them over about a half inch twice. Do it towards the wrong side and then the edge stitch folds down.

Now hem the bottom the same way and zigzag stitch along the diagonal sides. Once done, press the diagonal sides down about an inch to the wrong side and edge stitch them down.

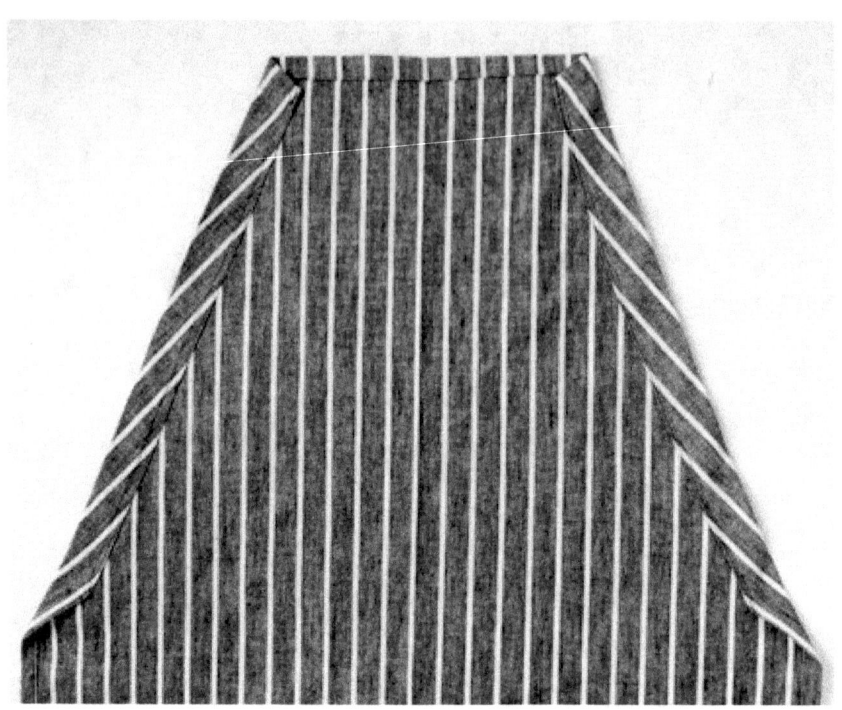

Time to attach the pocket. Press the top of the pocket down ½ inch twice towards the wrong side to hem and edge stitch the fold down. Then zigzag stitch along the three other sides of the fabric. Press the right and left sides towards the wrong side. Press the bottom edge up a half inch to the wrong side.

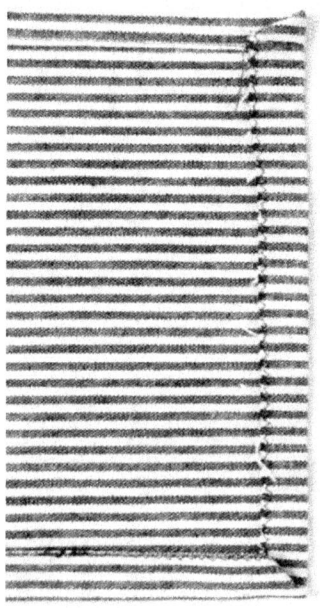

To form small miters, tuck the extra fabric of the corners inside the pressed folds. Then press the pocket flat. Now pin the bottom, right and left sides of the pocket to the main apron panel, about 2 ½ inches below the point where diagonal sides start. Ensure it's 4½ inches from both sides and that it's straight and centered.

To form a scant that is a 1-inch channel along the diagonal sides, press the diagonal sides down an inch to the wrong side and edge stitch them down. You will thread the cotton webbing through here later.

Then edge stitch on around the bottom, right and left sides. Mark vertically along the pocket using an erasable fabric Hera marker, 3½ inches from the left side. Then mark 3½ inches to the left of the mark.

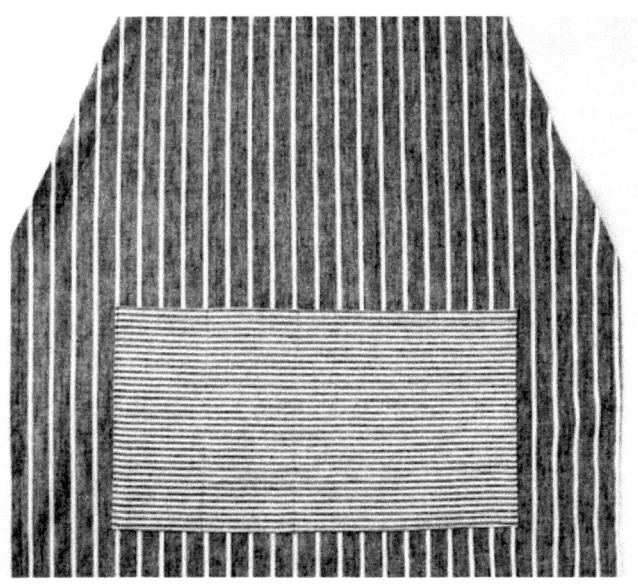

Sew along the marks in order to form two pocket divisions for the cooking tools. To add the tie, cut the cotton webbing to approximately 97 inches in length. To the wrong side, press the ends ½ inch twice, and edge stitch the folds down using the off-white thread.

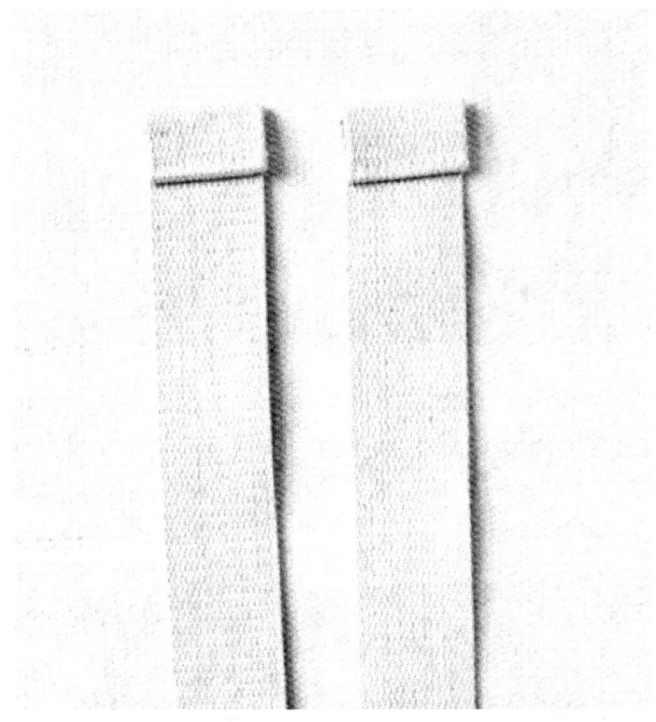

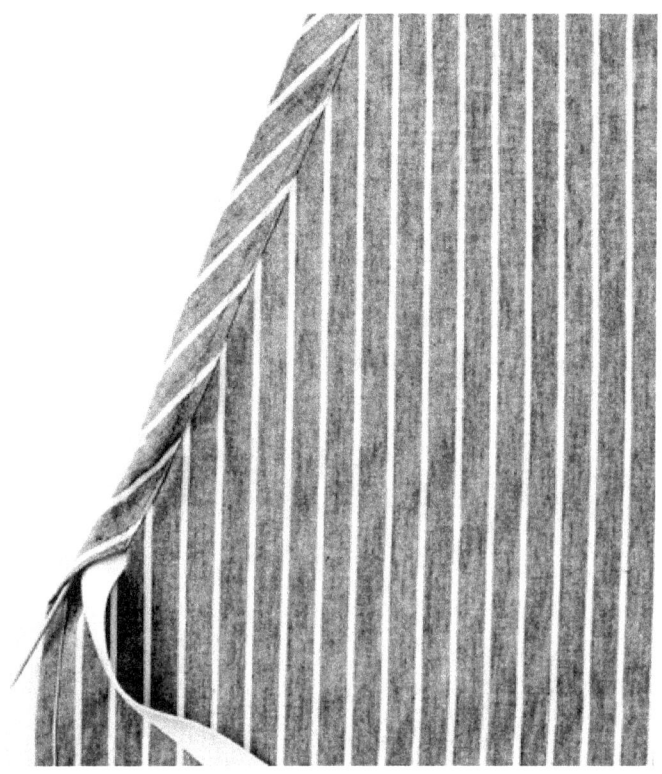

Pull one of end of the webbing through the bottom left diagonal side using a sharp object such as a knife; the wrong side of the apron should be facing up. Turn the webbing out at the top after reaching the top of the apron, and turn the apron to the wrong side.

You can now thread your webbing into the diagonal channel on the opposite side from the top while you pull this all the way through to the bottom of that channel. Take care not to twist it. Now pull the webbing to make both sides equal.

Chapter 4: Food Gift Ideas

Jack and Coke cake

What you'll need

- For the cake
- 1½ cups miniature marshmallows
- ½ teaspoon salt
- 1 teaspoon baking soda
- ¼ cup cocoa
- 2 cups flour
- 2 teaspoons vanilla
- 2 large eggs
- 1 ¾ cups sugar
- 1 cup butter
- ¼ cup whiskey or bourbon
- ¾ cup cola
- ½ cup plain yogurt

For the frosting

- 1 tablespoon vanilla

- 1 (16-ounce) package sugar, powdered

- 2 tablespoons whiskey or bourbon

- ¼ cup cocoa

- 1/3 cup cola

- ½ cup butter

How to make

First, preheat your oven to about 350° F, and then get all your ingredients ready for use. Combine whiskey, cola and the yoghurt in a small bowl and then set aside.

Into the microwave, soften your butter for about 10 seconds or so and then put into a large bowl. Beat the butter in a mixer on medium speed to form a creamy substance. Add in the sugar and continue to beat again until it's fully combined. Now add in the vanilla and eggs and then set aside.

Combine the rest of the ingredients and then add a half of this mixture to the butter mixture. Stir thoroughly until fully combined. Add the cola mixture, all at once and then continue to stir to mix well. Now add in the other half of dry ingredients and stir as usual.

Then stir in the marshmallows and then sub-divide the mixture among several Mason jars. Now bake the small jars in the pre-heated oven for about 30 minutes, or 45 minutes if you use the larger jars.

As the cake is baked, prepare the frosting by melting the butter, and then add in the cocoa and cola. Remove the mixture from heat and pour in whisky as well as the powdered sugar. Use a whisk to completely mix to smoothness. Spoon the frosting over the hot cakes. To serve, allow the cake to cool completely.

Veggie fries for men

What you'll need

- Food processor
- 3 baking trays
- 1-2 teaspoons Sriracha
- 2 tablespoons lemonaise or mayonnaise, low fat
- ½ cup flour or pancake mix
- 1 tablespoon olive oil|
- 2 large eggs
- 3 teaspoons Cajun seasoning, divided
- ¼ cup pine nuts
- ½ pound vegetables; zucchini, asparagus etc.

- ¼ cup Parmesan cheese

How to make

First, preheat the oven to 450° F and then get ready to make your breading. You can choose some pine nuts, Cajun seasoning, Panko and a little parmesan to get a nutty crunch. If using zucchini, first cut them into long wedged-shapes, and for asparagus, snap off the wooden ends first. Green beans would require trimming or snapping the ends before use.

You can try out a multigrain pancake mix to replace the ordinary flour and put it into the first tray. Into another tray, mix some eggs, olive eggs and Cajun seasoning and then set aside.

Have a third tray that should hold your panko mixture. Assemble your ingredients starting from the pancake mix, the egg wash and the breading.

Into a baking sheet that has been coated with cooking spray, place your breaded veggies and then bake for about 15-20 minutes. When ready, your veggies fries should turn brown and crispy.

Prepare a dipping sauce using Sriracha and mix it with lemonaise or mayonnaise.

Beef jerky

What you'll need

- 1 teaspoon cayenne pepper
- 3 tablespoons brown sugar
- 3 tablespoons sesame seeds
- 3 tablespoons onion powder
- 3 tablespoons garlic powder
- ½ cup Karo dark corn syrup
- 1 cup liquid smoke
- 2 cups thick, flavorful teriyaki sauce
- 2 cups Worcestershire sauce

- 2 cups soy sauce

- 5 lbs. lean brisket

How to make

Freeze the meat for about an hour to facilitate slicing. Start to slice the meat as thin as possible at ¼-inch thickness to ensure a longer-lasting jerky.

Combine 2 cups Worcestershire sauce, 2 cups soy sauce, ½ cup dark corn syrup, a cup of liquid smoke and 2 cups of teriyaki sauce. Add in 3 tablespoons brown sugar, 3 tablespoons sesame seeds, 3 tablespoons onion powder and 3 tablespoons garlic powder. Throw in a teaspoon of cayenne pepper, or a little more based on your preference.

Stir the mixture well, and then submerge the meat into the marinade. Cover or close the container and refrigerate for more than 24 hours.

After the meat has marinated, cook in the oven.

Position the meat onto racks, or put on an aluminum foil or hardware cloth. Set the temperature to between 160-180°F and crack open the oven's door by sticking a wooden spoon on the door. You should aim at drying the meat without cooking it.

Dry the meat for about 3 hours and ensure that you turn over the jerky. When done, it should be easy to rip off pieces of meat. Cool the meat for 24 hours to dry, and then store in sealed Ziploc bags. You can store the meat for up to 4-6 months without refrigeration.

Remote control cookies

What you'll need

- Actual remote
- Copier/printer
- Edible markers

How to make

Photocopy your remote and then cut it out. Put the cutout onto your cookie dough and then cut out the shape of the remote using a small knife. From the outline, fill and allow the cookie to dry.

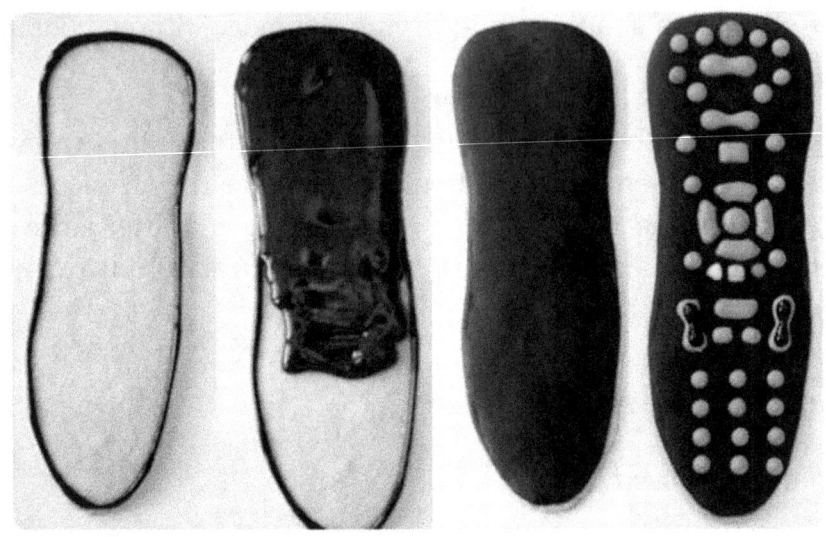

To make the buttons, ice the cookie with the actual colors of your remote. You can use edible markers with a fine tip in decorating the buttons. Complete your gift box by adding a candy at the bottom.

Big batch barbecue rub

What you'll need

- 1 tablespoon black pepper
- 4 teaspoons kosher salt
- 3 tablespoons ground coffee
- 3 tablespoons dried oregano
- 3 tablespoons brown sugar
- ½ cup paprika

How to make

Mix together the above ingredients and then store in an aright container for a maximum of two months.

Attach a gift tag to the container with the following instructions:

Two hours before cooking, coat 2 pounds of chicken, seafood, pork or beef with a tablespoon of olive oil. Then sprinkle with 2-4 tablespoons of the rub and cook as preferred.

Homemade honey curry mustard

What you'll need

- Salt to taste
- ½ tablespoon curry powder
- 1 tablespoon honey
- 1 tablespoon chopped shallots

- ¼ cup yellow mustard seeds
- ¼ cup brown mustard seeds
- ¼ cup rice vinegar
- ½ cup white wine

For thyme beer mustard

- Salt to taste
- ½ teaspoon fresh thyme, chopped
- 1 tablespoon shallots, chopped
- ¼ cup yellow mustard seeds
- ¼ cup brown mustard seeds
- 1/4 cup rice vinegar
- ½ cup beer

How to make

Place the ingredients of the two sets of recipes into two separate bowls, cover and put in the fridge overnight.

Blend the ingredients of each bowl to desired consistency in a blender. You can add more honey or salt and pepper if needed.

Transfer into airtight jar. The mustard will keep refrigerated for three months.

Chapter 5: Pampering Gift Ideas

Rosemary mint shaving cream

What you'll need

- 3-5 drops peppermint essential oil
- 10 drops rosemary essential oil
- ¼ cup jojoba or sweet almond oil
- 1/3 cup virgin coconut oil
- 1/3 cup shea butter

How to make

Over low heat, heat coconut oil and shea butter. Stir the mixture until well melted, and then remove from heat. Transfer the mixture into a heat safe bowl and then add in the other essential oils including jojoba oil. Stir to fully combine.

Refrigerate the mixture and then chill until it solidifies. When solid, remove from the fridge and then whip using a stand mixer or hand beater. When ready, you should have a light and fluffy substance. Spoon the cream into a jar, put a lid on and then store it in a cool, dry place.

Black and tan beer soap

What you'll need

- Vertical mold
- Super Pearly White Mica
- 1 ounce almond biscotti fragrance oil
- 3 ounces oatmeal stout fragrance oil
- 275 mL dark beer in 139 mL distilled water
- 6.5 ounces lye

- 14.8 ounces palm oil

- 15.3 ounces olive oil

- 14.8 ounces coconut oil

How to make

Boil your beer for about 5-10 minutes to cook out all the alcohol, ensuring you don't leave the beer unattended during the boiling period. Allow the beer to cool before using it in soap making.

Prepare your fragrance blend by mixing an ounce of almond biscotti fragrance oil and 3 ounces of oatmeal stout fragrance oil. Ensure you are safe from spills or vapors by wearing gloves and goggles, and keep away from children or pets.

Obtain your favorite dark beer, measure out about 9.2 ounces and then combine it with 4.7 ounces of distilled water.

Measure out a sufficient amount of lye and then add the lye slowly to the beer mixture in three batches. Do not add lye to the beer mixture quickly to avoid a violent reaction. Add lye continuously, until it's all added and dissolved. Allow the mixture to cool.

Now weigh and mix together olive oil, palm oil and coconut oil, making sure that solid oils are first melted in a stove or microwave. Very carefully, add the lye mixture into the oil mixture and then stick blend until a light trace is formed.

Subdivide the soap mixture into two portions, to have about 4 cups in each batch. To the first portion, add in a heaped tablespoon of Super Pearly White mica. Now use a stick blender to pulse and then hand stir all through. After the colorant has fully combined, add an ounce of your fragrance oil and whisk the mixture to combine.

To the second portion of uncolored soap batter, whisk the rest of the fragrance (about 3 ounce) and then quickly blend with the stick blend for about 10 seconds. Now pour the two portions of soap batter into their vertical molds to shape your soap.

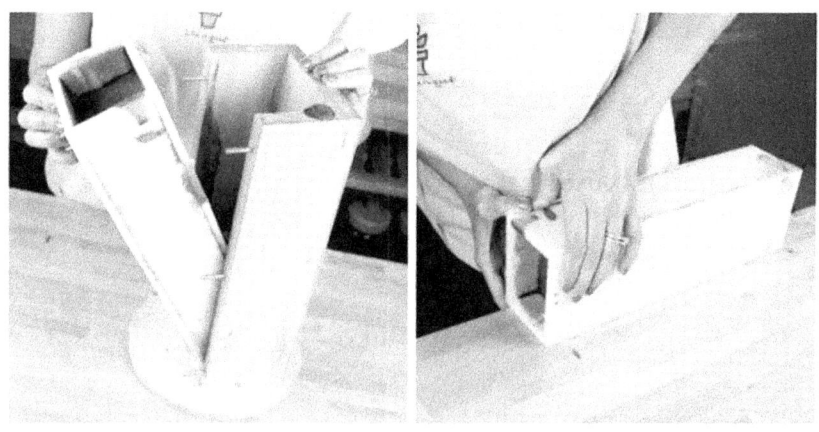

On the bottom of the soap, lift the divider from its resting spot and then twist it about 25 degrees. Pull it out gently in order to result into a zigzag design. Allow the soap to harden for a few days.

After about a week, unmold your soap by putting your soap on the side of the counter top and slowly pressing the sides down. Press and slide the sides off to prevent taking some soap pieces off with you.

Eucalyptus and vanilla bath salts

What you'll need

- Green food coloring
- 8 drops vanilla in jojoba oil
- 3 drops eucalyptus essential oil
- ½ cup baking soda
- 1 cup Epsom salt

How to make

Into a large sealable plastic bag, combine essential oils, baking soda and Epsom salt. If desired, add a drop of food coloring to add color to the bath salt.

Now seal the bag and massage the contents using your hands to fully blend the ingredients.

Once done, transfer the bath salt into a plastic bag in a container with a lid. When using, one spoon per bath is enough.

DIY fragrance made with vodka

What you'll need

- Perfume bottle
- Measuring cup with spout
- Dropper or baster
- Large glass jar with a tight-fitting lid
- 3 tablespoons vodka
- 5 drops glycerin
- 3 varieties of essential oil, 25 drops total
- 2 cups distilled water

How to make

Choose various essential oils such as orange, eucalyptus and lemon. Measure distilled water with a measuring cup and put into a large glass jar. Add vodka to the water, followed by 5 drops of glycerin, and combine fully.

Add in 25 drops of essential oil mixture and stir; mix well and then transfer into a tight fitting lidded container. You can use more essential oil if needed.

Store the jar with the fragrance in a dark, cool place for at least 12 hours. Then shake the contents to combine them, and transfer into a perfume bottle using a baster or dropper.

Chamomile & neroli beer soap

What you'll need

- ounces chamomile flowers
- 0.25 ounces Roman chamomile essential oil
- 1.75 ounces neroli fragrance oil
- 4.8 ounces lye/sodium hydroxide
- 12 fluid ounces Sierra Nevada Pale Ale, cold and flat
- 1.8 ounce illipe butter
- 7.2 ounces sustainable palm oil
- 7 ounces 76° melting point coconut oil
- 3 ounces castor oil
- 8 ounces rice bran oil
- 9 ounces olive oil

How to make

Weigh out the lye using your digital kitchen scale and then pour it into the beer a little at a time as you continue to stir with each pour. Continue to add lye until the entire amount has fully combined with the beer, and then set aside to cool.

Now weigh out the oils and butter and put into a stainless steel pot to melt on a stove over medium heat. Once all the oils have melted, remove from heat and cool to around 100° F.

Ensure both the lye and the oil mixture have the same temperature of about 100° F and then pour the beer and lye mixture into the soap making oil. Use a stick blender to mix until you obtain a light trace.

Now stir in the chamomile flowers and fragrances and mix fully. Once mixed, pour into a prepared soap mold, cover and store in a warm place for around 24 hours. Then remove the soap from your mold and slice into bars.

Let your soap cure for 3-6 weeks before sending your gift for use. Be sure to use cold, flat beer for the recipe.

Chapter 6: Miscellaneous Crafts Ideas

Shrinky Dink gift

What you'll need

- Keychain key rings
- Tie tack backings
- Super glue
- Photo of your child
- Shrinky Dink kit

How to make

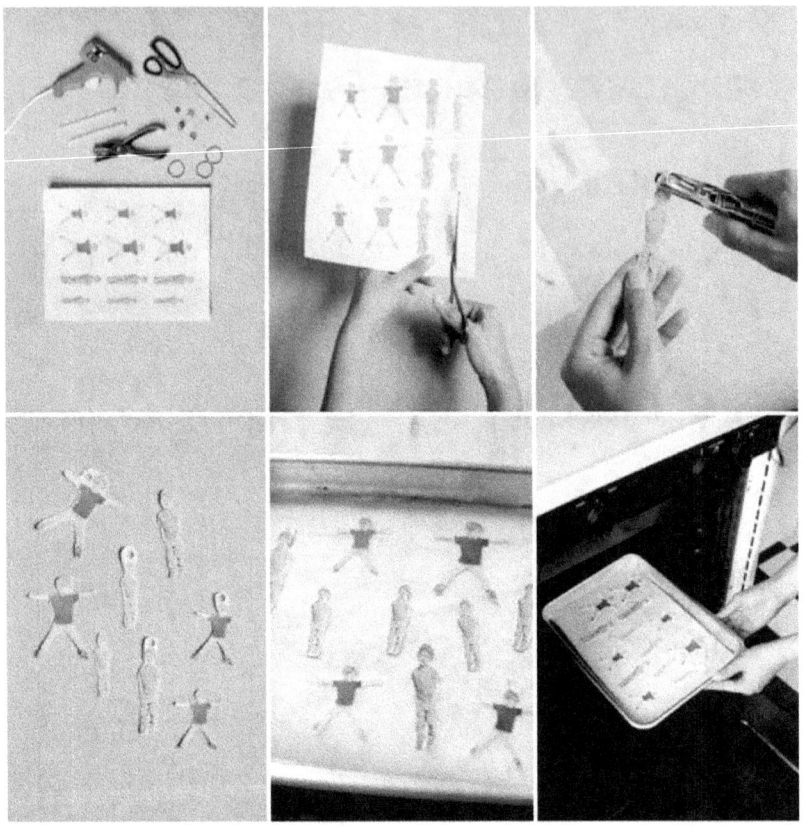

Go to your computer and size your photos, ensuring they are twice as big as would be in the Shrinky Dink. Print out your designed images directly onto your plastic Shrinky Dink sheets and then cut the images out. For the key chains, leave a little paper bit at the very top to make it possible to punch a hole through.

Preheat the oven to about 325° F and then line a baking sheet with parchment paper. Then arrange your Shrinky Dinks in layers and bake them for about 3-5 minutes.

When baked, allow them to fully cool and then apply superglue on the materials to be attached. These could include key rings or tie tack backings.

Tripod camping stool

What you'll need

- Knife
- Rags
- Small socket wrench
- Screwdriver

- Drill
- Center-finder
- Sander
- *Materials*
- Leather/heavy material
- Finish
- 3 brass 1" wood screws
- 3 brass finishing washers
- 3 brass washers
- 2 brass acorn nuts
- 1.5" eye-hole bolt
- 1 brass 2.75" bolt
- 3 1 1/8" birch hardwood dowels, enough for three 24" pieces

How to make

Cut the dowels to about 24 inches and then drill a hole through each, about 10.5 inches from the top of each leg. Determine the center of the legs top and then drill a little pilot hole for the screws to mount seat on. The pilot hole is needed to stop the legs from splitting. Then sand each of your legs smooth, both at the top and bottom. Make sure you don't shorten any of the legs when rounding.

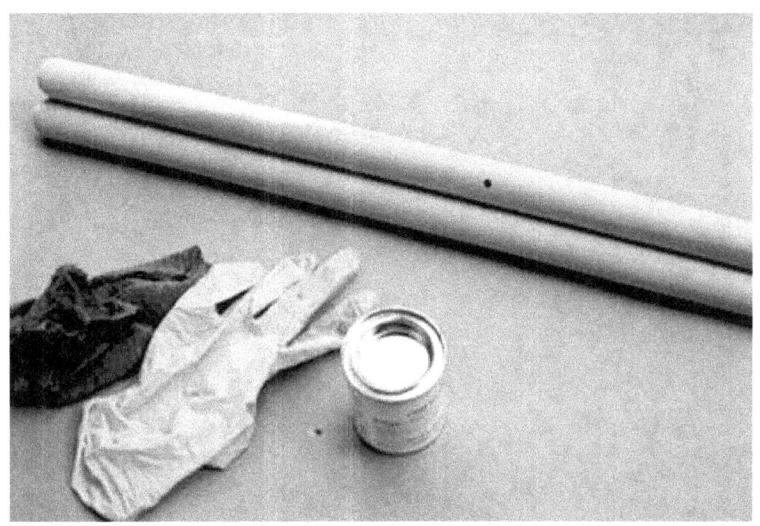

To complete the legs, just apply your desired finish and then set them aside to dry.

Start working on the seat material from leather or heavy canvas seat among other materials. The material you adopt should be firmly reinforced and heavy to accommodate the amount of pressure exerted during sitting.

If desired, you can leave a tab to attach the carrying strap during travelling and camping. You can also attach your stool to a closure strap to help keep it from popping open during storage or transportation. If using a leather piece, you may edge and treat the smooth surfaces using carnauba wax.

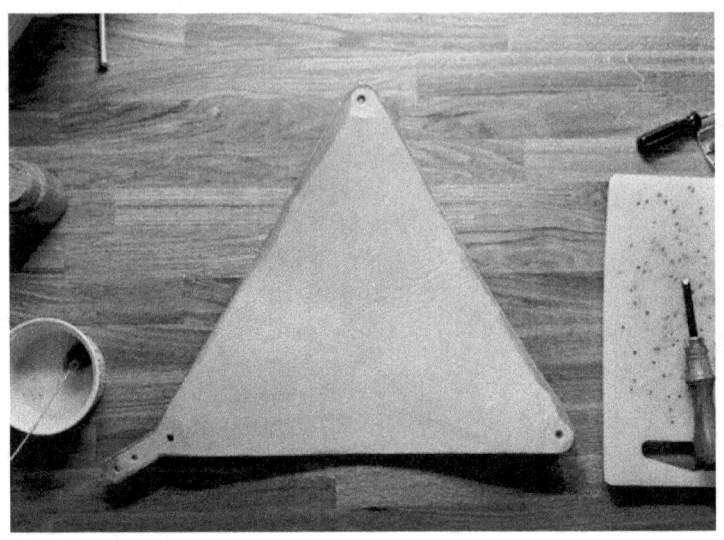

Confirm whether the legs are dry and then assemble the structure. Using some bolts, just thread 2 of the legs, with the eye-bolt located at the center. Both ends of the bolts should have washers, with acorn nut attached. Then feed the eye-hole bolt after the legs are secure. Use a washer to attach together with an acorn nut. Now use a socket wrench to make the two acorns firm and secure.

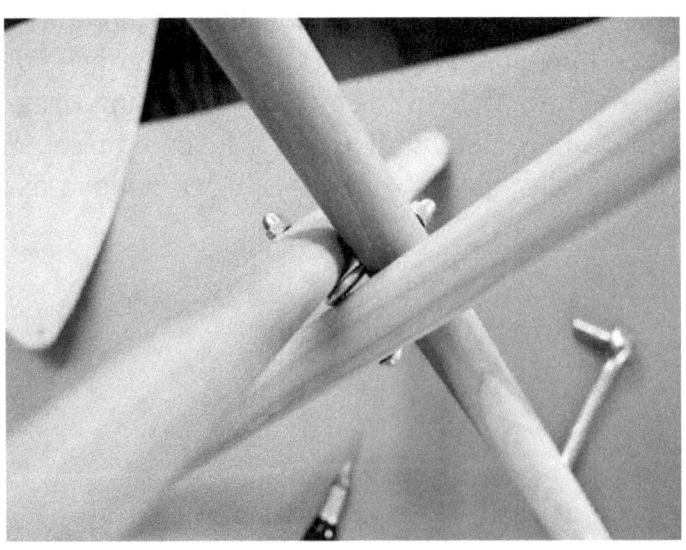

Using a wood screw and a large finishing washer, attach the seat to each leg without over tightening and stripping out the holes. This is because a lot of pressure would be applied on these points. Make sure the whole set-up is secure and then take your seat.

Bicycle frame lunch bag

What you'll need

- 8x8" square fabric
- 8x13" rectangle fabric
- 3x22" strip
- Velcro

How to make

Select a sturdy material to use, such as canvas, vinyl or oil cloth. When sewing, your seam allowances should be ½ inch all through.

Sew the 3x22" strip around its exterior of the front side of the bag. To turn the strip and the square in the next direction, just position your sewing machine needle down and the pivot at the corners.

To form a rolled hem, just fold over ¼ inch and another ¼ inch across the front's top as well as the bag's sides. Now sew it down. Canvas can hold a finger crease well, therefore making the rolling of the hem easier.

Sew the back on, and then rotate it at its corners once more. Now hem your flap by folding in the corner tips before you roll the sides.

Obtain a Velcro cable to use in tying the bag to the bicycle during use. The cables are extra thin and very easy to sew. From their thickness, they don't interfere with cabling on a bicycle.

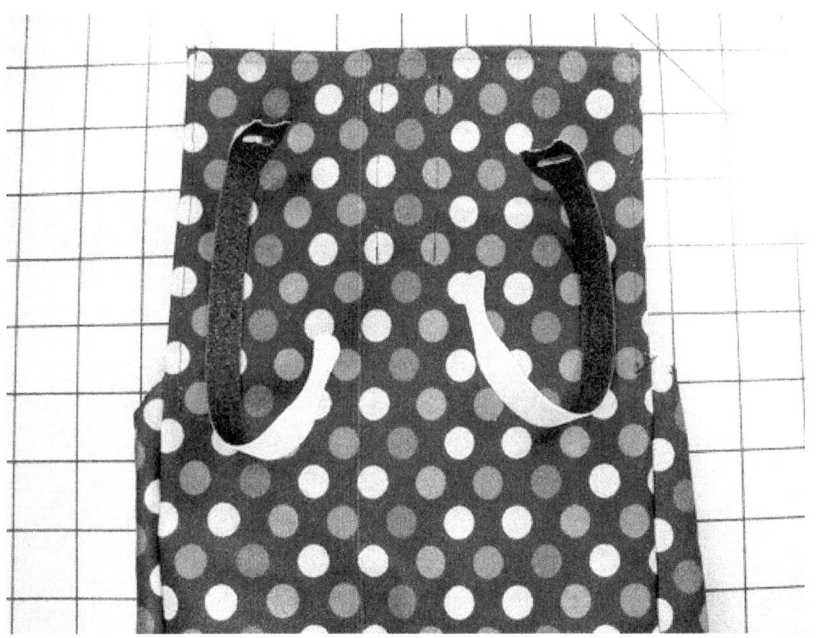

Sew the two Velcro strips to the top of the flap to be used during connection to the top tube of a bicycle.

You need to sew one more strap to the bottom of your bag's sides, to help connect the bag to the seat tube. You may also need to sew an additional Velcro cable to the front side and a flap to maintain the flap closed. This helps to prevent flapping when the bicycle is moving fast.

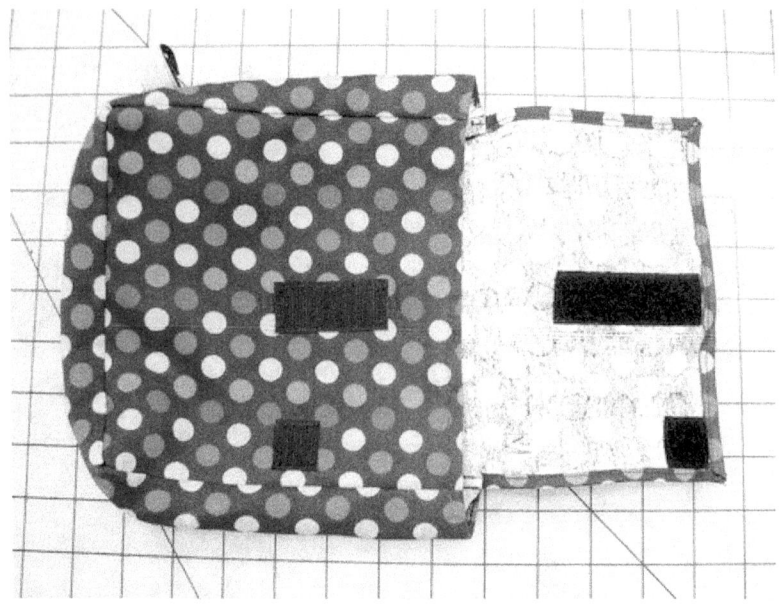

You are now done with the sandwich bike bag.

Simple stitched vinyl wallet

What you'll need

- Vinyl for outer piece = 4.5x6.5"
- Vinyl for each pocket = 4.5x2.5"
- Sewing machine
- Ruler

How to make

Measure out the vinyl fabric for your wallet or adjust the sizes based on your preference to make recipe card holders or business card holders.

Stitch the outer piece with contrasting thread.

Now pick from the last stitch from the reverse side. Do this until you are able to pull the thread from the front back through. When done, knot the loose ends and secure all the stitches.

Finish the wallet by sewing two pockets, stitching around all edges of the wallet. When done, use a rotary cutter to remove any overhanging bits, and then tidy the edges using a ruler.

Homemade leather wallet

What you'll need

- 2 square feet leather material, 2 ounce thickness
- Stitching thread, TEX138 - TEX270
- 2 ball point stitching needles
- Awl or ice pick
- 2 push pins
- Straight rule
- Razor blade
- Scissors
- How to make
- Design your own pattern or use the template below, print it and then cut into paper patterns.

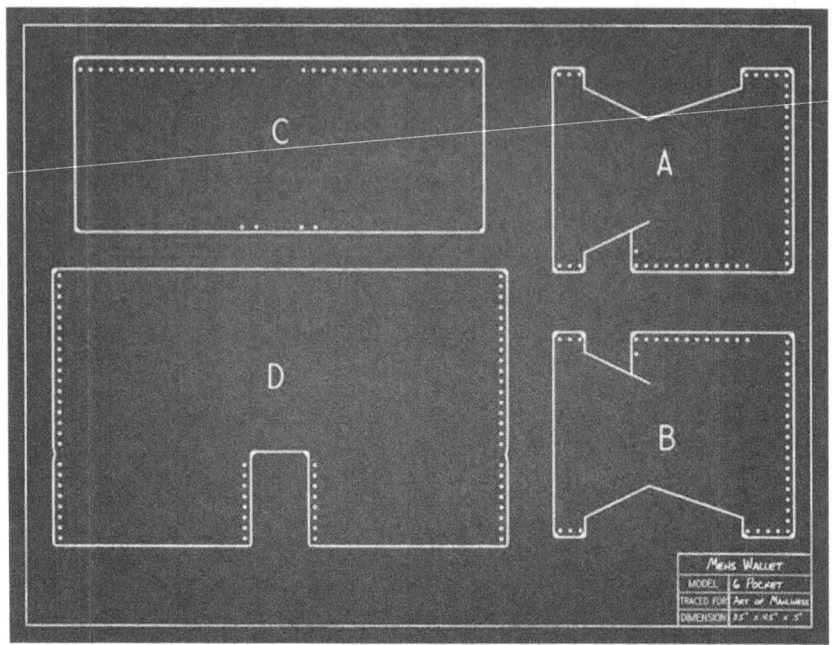

Then trace the design onto leather sheet.

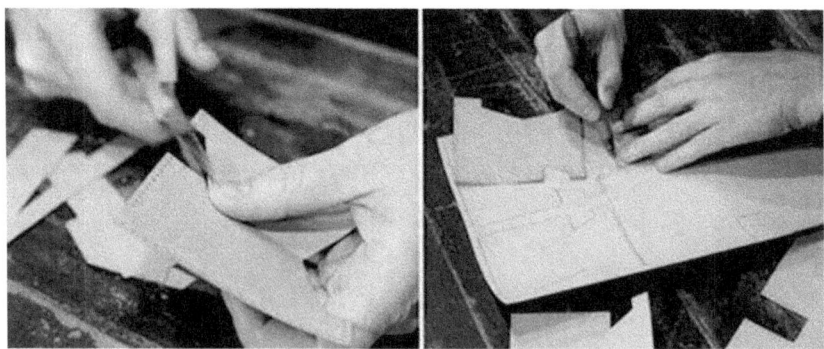

Cut the pieces carefully out of the leather and ensure that you cut the lines cleanly by use of a rotary bade alongside a straightedge or ruler.

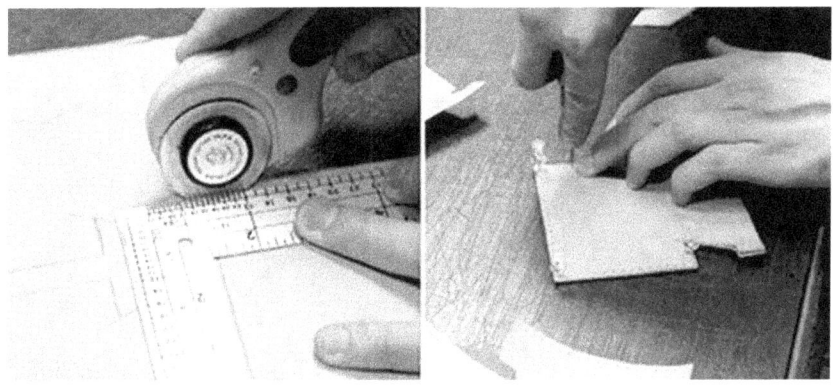

Punch the stitching holes into the leather after cutting out the pieces, and use push pins to tack the paper pattern onto the leather piece. Also, use an awl or an ice pick to make evenly spaced holes. Your holes should be large enough to allow thread and needles through without resistance.

Prepare to assemble your pieces. Layer the smaller pieces A and B on top of C to go on top of D. Then fold the leather to see where the holes line up. You can crease the leather thoroughly to make the stitching process faster.

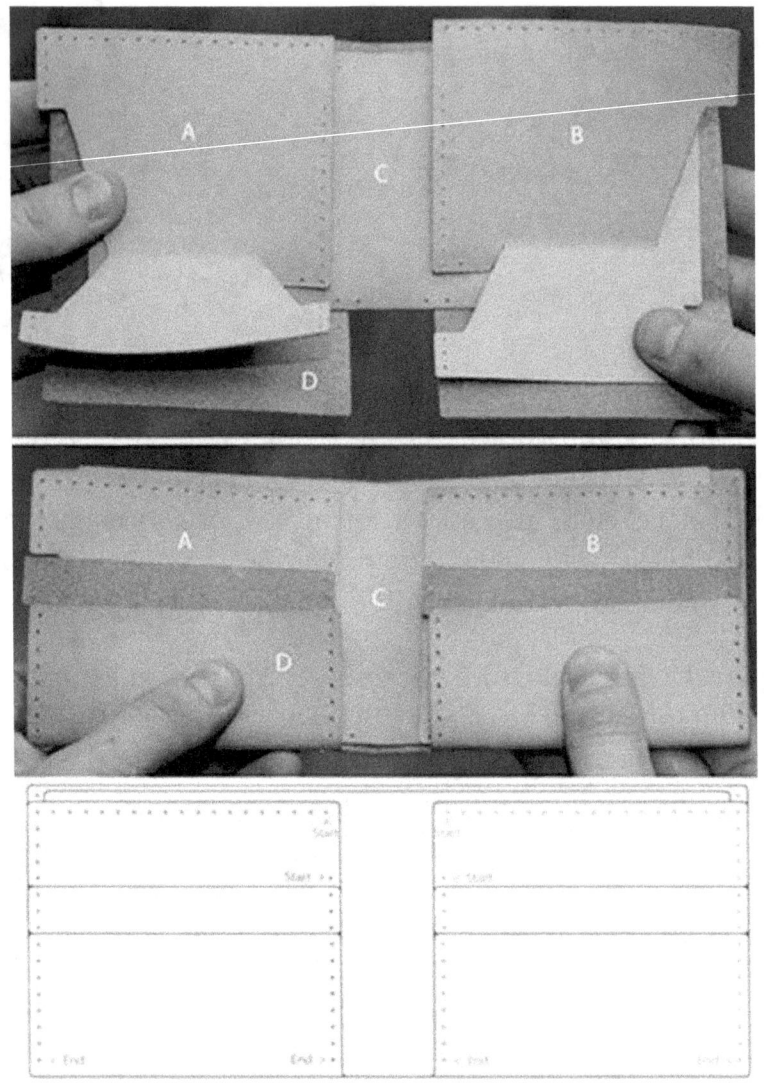

Use the saddle stitching method where one thread and two needles are used, one needle being at the end of the thread. Align the holes to bind the two pieces together and then weave two needles through the aligned hole.

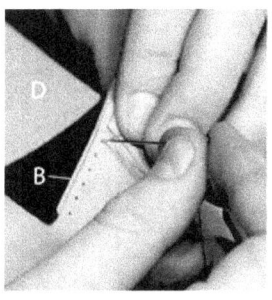 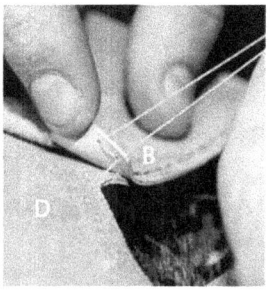 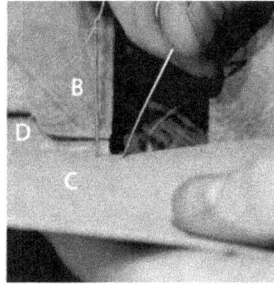

Start from the blue stitching path, using 2 feet of thread. At the starting point of piece B, pass one of your needles through the first hole. Now pull through until you get equal length of thread on each side of your leather. From the same side of the leather, pick one of the needles and start it through the next hole. Then start the other needle through the same hole but on the opposite side.

Now grasp the 2 needles and pull through until the stitch is nice and tight. Begin binding piece D to B after you reach the 4th hole. At the end point, pass the two needles to the back side and weave the threads. Both needles should stick out of the back of side B. Take the needles from the backside of B and then add on piece C.

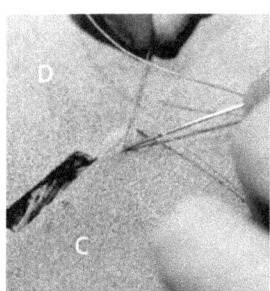 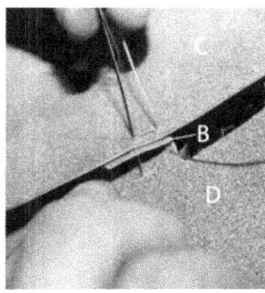 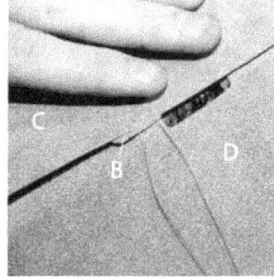

Weave the needles to the end of the path between the two aligned holes B and C. Now check whether the stitching is good and firm along the blue path, and make any adjustments if required. Then you can tie off the two threads through three consecutive overhand knots.

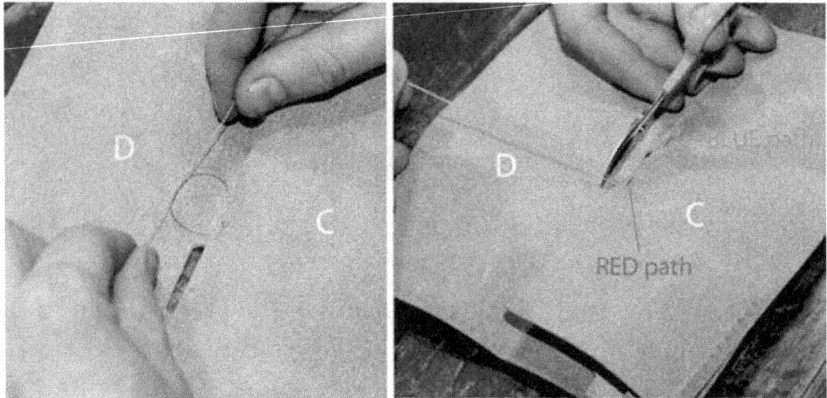

The red path from the illustration represents the inverse shape, but follows a similar method as blue path. Follow the same routine to stitch piece A to D and C and tie off the red path. Leave about a quarter inch of remnant thread.

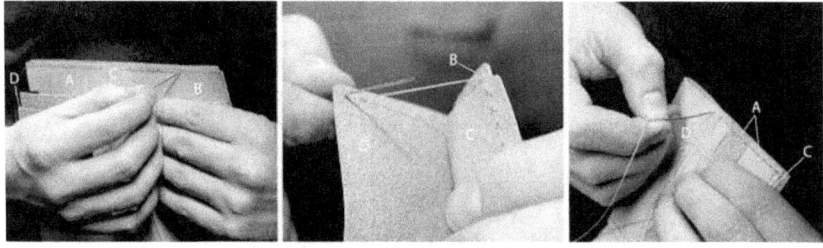

Now move on to stitch the green and yellow paths. Spend the first 18 stitches of the path binding A and B to C. Include piece D into the stitching after reaching the corners and close up the side of the wallet.

The yellow and green stitching paths' end point should take you to the fold of part D. Bring the threads through the middle after reaching the corners, and tie them off using three knots. Then cut the remaining thread and finally tuck the knot into the corner fold.

Swiss Army key ring

What you'll need

- Glue to bond wood to metal
- Ten #8 machine screw washers
- Thin sheet metal (about 2 x 3.75")
- Two #8 machine screws, 3/4" long
- Wood stain

- Two #8 machine screw lock nuts

- Polyurethane

- Two pieces of wood (about 1 x 3.75 x 1/8" each)

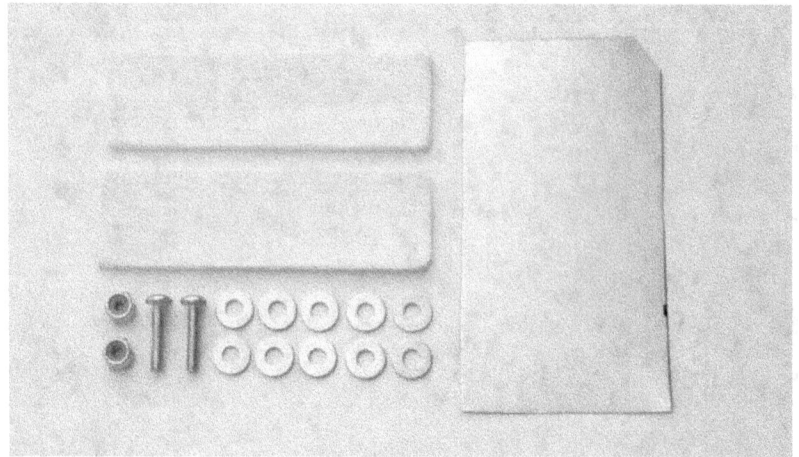

- *Tools*

- Ruler

- Pencil

- Small binder clamps

- Sandpaper/sanding block

- Tin snips

- Drill and bit set

How to make

Start by cutting the sheet metal and wood to shape. Then trace a semicircle onto each end of the wood pieces using any rounded object. Cut along the outline you have traced using a knife or saw.

Onto the sheet metal, trace the shape of the wood pieces and use a pair of tin snips to cut out two pieces of sheet metal. The pieces should be smaller than the outlines.

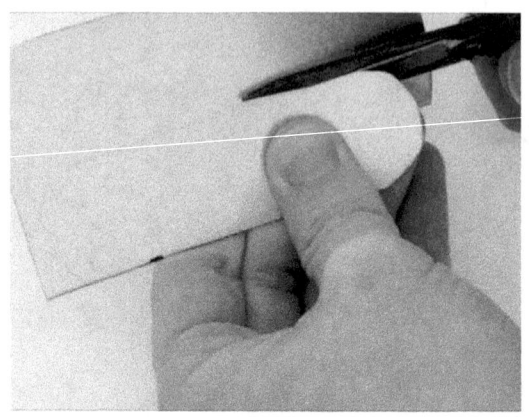

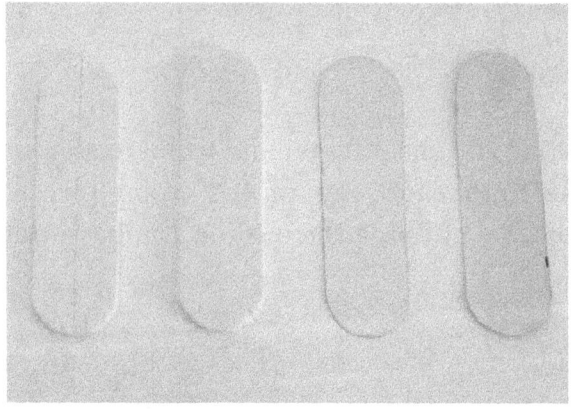

To drill the bolt holes, make a stack of 2 pieces of wood and 2 pieces of metal. Ensure that the pieces are centered and then use a binder clamp to support them. Then mark the centers of the semi-circles on each of the ends to be approximately 2.75 inches apart.

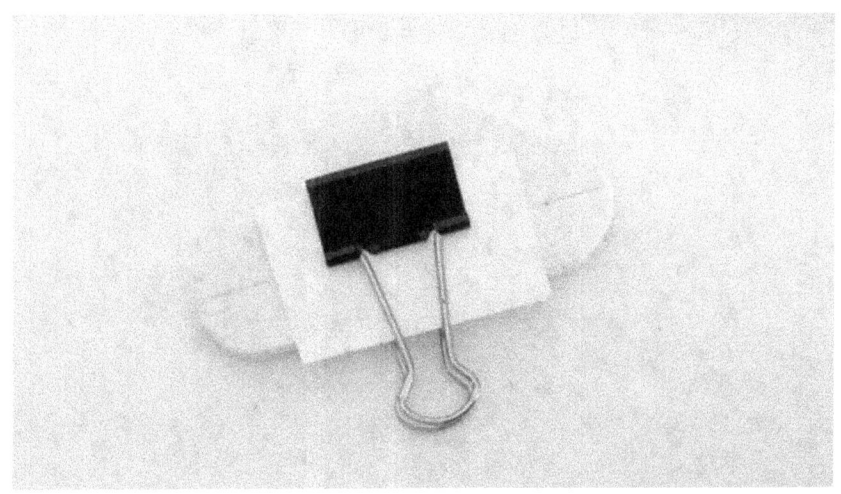

At one of these points, drill through the four layers using a 3/16" drill bit and insert a screw into the hole to help the layers stay lined up. Drill the second hole and remove the two metal pieces.

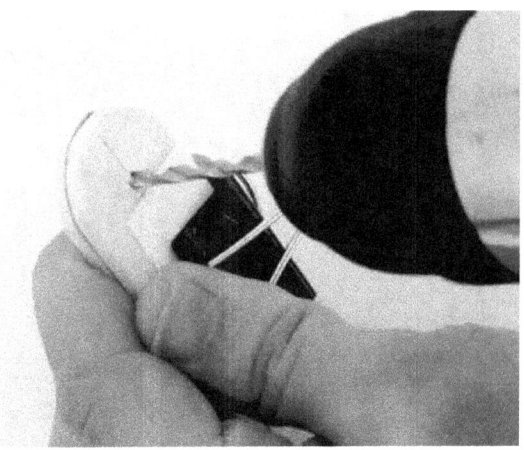

Re-drill the holes in the wood pieces to ensure the holes can hold the head of the machine screw together with the lock nut. You can wrap the pieces of wood in tape to avoid possible splitting when you are drilling larger holes. Once done, sand the surfaces smooth.

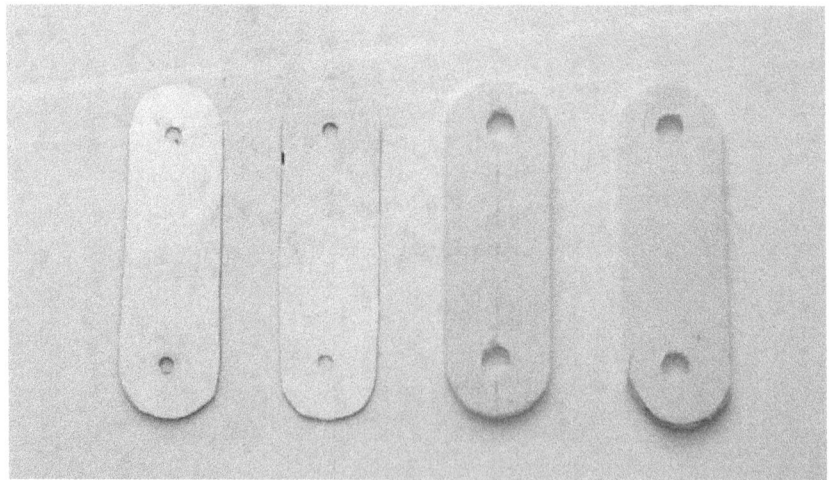

Get ready to assemble the frame by inserting the machine screws through the holes in the metal pieces. Add in the washers and keys, such as 4 keys and 5 washers, which should fit on a ¾ inch screw. Three washers and two keys should also fit onto a ½ inch screw, while 6 keys and 7 washers should fit on an inch screw. To fit in, start with sheet metal, then washer, key, washer and progress this way to finish with sheet metal.

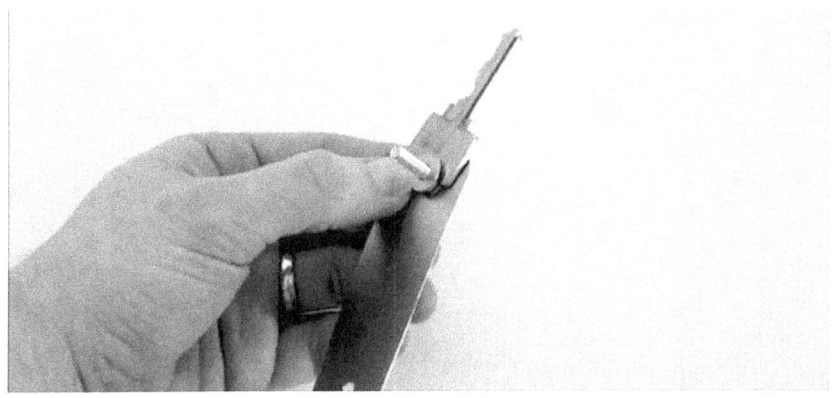

You can also save space by doing away with the washers, though the keys would be stuck to each other. Once done, add another piece of sheet metal and use the two lock nuts to tighten the design.

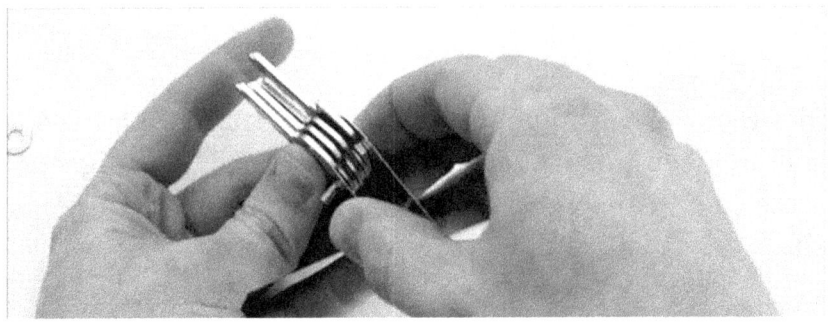

To glue on the wooden panels, just apply a thin layer of glue to the exterior side of the plate and press on the wooden panel. Repeat the process for the other panel and then hold everything together using binder clamps while waiting for the glue to dry. If needed, add another layer or two of card stock to avoid denting the wood panels with the clamps.

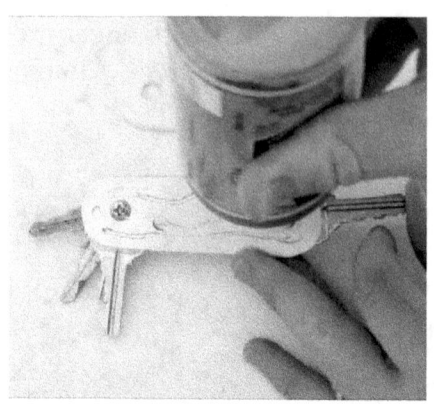

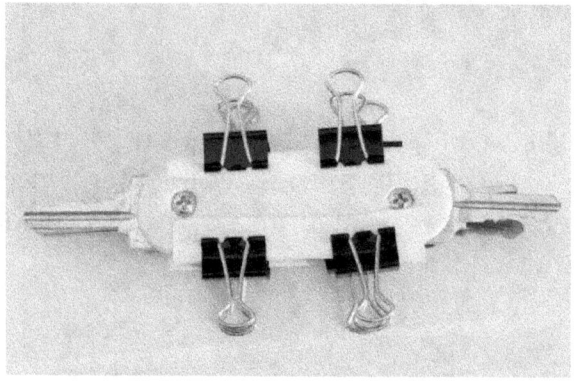

If desired, you can apply stain and polyurethane to the wooden panels and let it dry to make it more unique. Obtain a piece of cheesecloth to apply the stain and later apply the polyurethane using a sponge brush.

This key holder design saves space in that keys are placed parallel to each other and don't fan out, and the double folding design enables the blades from both key sets to fit within the handle.

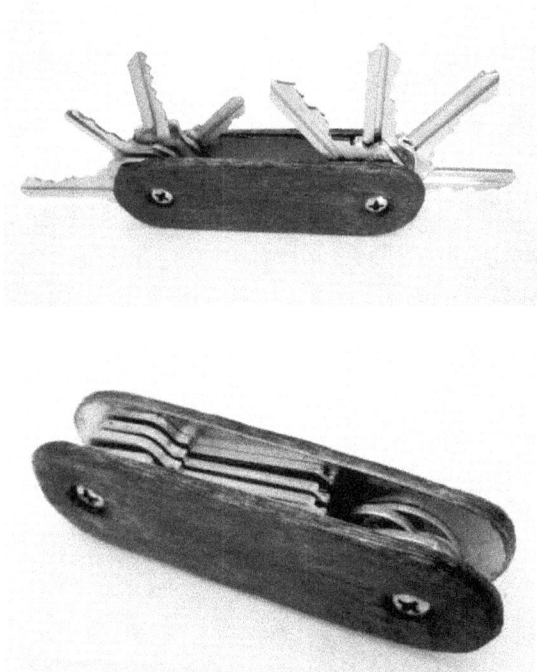

Conclusion

Giving your father a simple handmade gift is one of the best things that you can ever do. He's more likely to appreciate such a gift than some watch or cologne from the mall that you just wrap and hand to him. A handmade gift adds some personality and makes him appreciate the gift even more. So start making the gifts outlined in this book and put a smile on your father's face.

Key Takeaways from this Book

#1: After reading this book, you will see the relationship between you and your environment, and learn ways of recycling items you don't use anymore to make gifts.

#2: This book can motivate you to continue with craftsmanship, to become more creative, or even to develop a business out of it.

#3: Starting out will definitely be challenging, especially if you not into DIY kind of things. However, over time, you will get the hang of it and become better.

#4: You can save a lot of money by simply making handmade gifts as compared to buying gifts.

How to Put This Information into Action

1. Consider the kind of feedback you would give after receiving a DIY gift, and then use this analysis to figure out the most suitable gift to design. You don't need to offer impractical gifts or gifts out of context.

2. Also consider the nature of the gift to present this Father's Day to ensure that it addresses the expectations or needs it is meant to. Your recipient should be interested in your gift.

3. Before you try out any of the projects illustrated here, it's best to be aware of your level of technical know-how. You don't need to attempt projects you can't handle.

4. Insofar as handmade products are cheaper, you need to balance cost for the item against other parameters such as time required and availability of raw materials. This can help you in making an informed decision on which DIY gift idea to try.

Preview of Essential Oils and Aromatherapy: A Beginner's Guide to Making Essential Oils to Improve Your Mental and Physical Well-Being

Essential Oils for Physical Wellbeing

Using essential oils for skincare and hair care

Essential oil lore is a vast well of knowledge that science has barely touched. There are so many uses of essential oils, with new ones coming out every day. Below are just a few ways you can use essential oils to care for your skin and hair.

Body spray

Combine 5-10 drops of your favorite essential oil with 4 ounces of water in a spray bottle and shake well. Spray as you would a normal body spray.

Note: When using citrus essential oil, don't spray it on your face: citrus oil is photosensitive that makes your skin susceptible to sunburn.

Shampoo

Use lavender cedar wood to treat an itchy scalp by adding a few drops to your shampoo. When you want fuller hair, add rosemary essential oil to your shampoo.

Skin cream

If you want anti-aging support, add two drops of rosemary or rose essential oil to your skin cream.

DIY body oil

Add 5 drops of your favorite skin-safe essential oil to a carrier oil such as olive, borage seed, apricot kernel, wheat germ, or sweet almond. Use liberally every day, and remember to test for skin sensitivity.

In your bathwater

When you are adding essential oils to your bathwater, I strongly suggest you keep away from culinary essential oils such as lemongrass, peppermint, and cinnamon, just to point out a few, because they might cause skin irritation.

To your bathtub, add 5 drops of a skin-safe essential oil.

To download the rest of this book, please click here.

More Books You Might Like

Household DIY: *Save Time and Money with Do It Yourself Hints and Tips on Furniture, Clothes, Pests, Stains, Residues, Odors and More!*

DIY Household Hacks: *Save Time and Money with Do It Yourself Tips and Tricks for Cleaning Your House*

Essential Oils: Essential Oils & Aromatherapy for Beginners: *Proven Secrets to Weight Loss, Skin Care, Hair Care & Stress Relief Using Essential Oil Recipes*

Apple Cider Vinegar for Beginners: *An Apple Cider Vinegar Handbook with Proven Secrets to Natural Weight Loss, Optimum Health and Beautiful Skin*

Body Butter Recipes: *Proven Formula Secrets to Making All Natural Body Butters that Will Hydrate and Rejuvenate Your Skin*

If the links do not work, for whatever reason, you can simply search for these titles on the Amazon website to find them.

Your Free Bonus

As a way of thanking you for your purchase, I'm offering you an opportunity to sign up and be a part of an exclusive book list where members get advanced notice on high-quality books.

To be part of this exclusive club, click on the link below:

https://docs.google.com/forms/d/1ttDqtdRjOeAEtA-BKnq5Hw668vjQSoVWcXCGQ8z9frA/viewform

www.ingramcontent.com/pod-product-compliance
Lightning Source LLC
Chambersburg PA
CBHW071419070526
44578CB00003B/620